Security
Welfare, Crime and Society

This book is part of a series published by Open University Press in association with The Open University. The three books in the *Welfare, Crime and Society* series are:

Social Justice: Welfare, Crime and Society (edited by Janet Newman and Nicola Yeates)

Security: Welfare, Crime and Society (edited by Allan Cochrane and Deborah Talbot)

Community: Welfare, Crime and Society (edited by Gerry Mooney and Sarah Neal)

This publication forms part of the Open University course *Welfare, crime and society* (DD208). Details of this and other Open University courses can be obtained from the Student Registration and Enquiry Service, The Open University, PO Box 197, Milton Keynes, MK7 6BJ, United Kingdom; tel. +44 (0)845 300 6090; email general-enquiries@open.ac.uk

Alternatively, you may visit the Open University website at http://www.open.ac.uk where you can learn more about the wide range of courses and packs offered at all levels by The Open University.

To purchase a selection of Open University course materials visit http://www.ouw.co.uk, or contact Open University Worldwide Ltd, Walton Hall, Milton Keynes MK7 6AA, United Kingdom for a brochure, tel. +44 (0)1908 858785; fax +44 (0)1908 858787; email ouw-customer-services@open.ac.uk

Security

Welfare, Crime and Society

Edited by Allan Cochrane and Deborah Talbot

Open University Press in association with The Open University

Open University Press
McGraw-Hill Education
McGraw-Hill House
Shoppenhangers Road
Maidenhead
Berkshire
England
SL6 2QL

Email: enquiries@openup.co.uk
world wide web: www.openup.co.uk

and Two Penn Plaza, New York, NY 10121-2289, USA

First published 2008

A catalogue record of this book is available from the British Library.

ISBN 0 3352 2932 8 *paperback*

ISBN 978 0 3352 2932 1 *paperback*

ISBN 0 3352 2931 X *hardback*

ISBN 978 0 3352 2931 4 *hardback*

Library of Congress Cataloguing-in-Publication Data

CIP data applied for

Edited and designed by The Open University.

Typeset in India by Alden Prepress Services, Chennai.

Printed and bound in the United Kingdom by Bell & Bain Ltd., Glasgow.

1.1

Contents

Notes on contributors

Allan Cochrane is Professor of Urban Studies at The Open University. He is author of *Understanding Urban Policy* (Blackwell, 2007) and (with John Allen and Doreen Massey) of *Rethinking the Region* (Routledge, 1998), as well as editor (with John Clarke and Sharon Gewirtz) of *Comparing Welfare States* (Sage, 2001).

Ross Fergusson is Senior Lecturer in Social Policy at The Open University. He is co-editor of *Restorative Justice: Crucial Issues* (Sage, 2003) and *Ordering Lives: Family, Work and Welfare* (Routledge, 2000), and publishes in the fields of youth policy and youth criminal justice.

Yvonne Jewkes is Professor of Criminology at the University of Leicester. She has published ten books on various aspects of media and crime, cyber crime, and imprisonment including, most recently, *Crime Online* (Willan, 2007) and *Handbook on Prisons* (Willan, 2007). She is co-editor of *Crime, Media, Culture: an international journal* (Sage), and series editor of the Sage Key Approaches to Criminology series.

Jane McCarthy is Reader in Family Studies at The Open University. Her key books include *Mothers and Their Children: A Feminist Sociology of Childrearing* (Sage, 1994), *Feminist Dilemmas in Qualitative Research: Public Knowledge and Private Lives* (co-edited with Rosalind Edwards; Sage, 1998), *Making Families: Moral Tales of Parenting and Step-Parenting* (with Rosalind Edwards and Val Gillies; Sociology Press, 2003) and *Young People's Experiences of Loss and Bereavement: Towards an Inter-Disciplinary Approach* (Open University Press, 2006).

John Muncie is Professor of Criminology and co-director of the International Centre for Comparative Criminological Research at The Open University. His recent books include *Youth and Crime (*3rd edition, Sage, 2009), *The Sage Dictionary of Criminology (*2nd edition with Eugene McLaughlin; Sage, 2006), *Youth Crime and Justice (*with Barry Goldson; Sage, 2006), *Comparative Youth Justice (*with Barry Goldson; Sage, 2006) and *The Student Handbook of Criminal Justice and Criminology* (with David Wilson; Cavendish, 2004).

Sarah Neal is Senior Lecturer in Social Policy at The Open University. Her books include *The Making of Equal Opportunities Policies in Universities* (Open University Press, 1998), *The New Countryside: Ethnicity, Nation and Exclusion in Contemporary Rural Britain* (edited with Julian Agyeman; The Policy Press, 2006), *Rural Identities: Ethnicity and Community in the Contemporary English Countryside* (Ashgate, 2008) and *Race, Multiculture and Social Policy* (Palgrave Macmillan, 2010).

Deborah Talbot is Lecturer in Criminology at The Open University and author of *Regulating the Night: Race, Culture and Exclusion in the Making of the Night-time Economy* (Ashgate, 2007).

Nicola Yeates is Senior Lecturer in Social Policy at The Open University. Her recent books include *Globalisation and Social Policy* (Sage, 2001), *Understanding Global Social Policy* (The Policy Press, 2008) and *Migrant Workers and Globalising Care Economies: Explorations in Global Care Chains* (Palgrave Macmillan, 2009). She is co-editor of *Global Social Policy: an interdisciplinary journal of public policy and social development* (Sage) and a member of the international advisory board of *Translocations: The Irish migration, race and social transformation review* (www.imrstr.dcu.ie).

Series preface

Security: Welfare, Crime and Society is the second of three books in a new series of textbooks published by Open University Press in association with The Open University. The series, entitled *Welfare, Crime and Society*, is designed to provide a social scientific understanding of the complex and fascinating entanglements between the worlds of social welfare and crime control. At the heart of the series is the suggestion that it is difficult to draw a clear line between social welfare and crime control. These entanglements are examined in respect of ideas, institutions, policies and practices – and their effects and impacts. The series extends beyond national borders to look at other societies and the policy concerns and developments that link them to present-day United Kingdom. The series uses different sources of evidence to understand these trends and their effects, and it examines how evidence is mobilised in the course of research, evaluation and policymaking.

The three books in this series are as follows:

■ *Social Justice: Welfare, Crime and Society*, edited by Janet Newman and Nicola Yeates. This book explores ways of defining and enacting social justice in the context of social welfare and crime control strategies. It examines how the notion of social justice informs experiences and understandings of the social world, why it appeals to so many people as a mobilising ideal for social change and policy reform, and how it shapes claims, demands and actions people take in the pursuit of the 'good society'.

■ *Security: Welfare, Crime and Society*, edited by Allan Cochrane and Deborah Talbot. This book focuses on the ways in which security as an idea, an ideal and a practice can shed light on the entanglements and intersections between welfare and crime, and the ambiguities, tensions and contradictions that arise from them. The book is concerned specifically with the increasingly blurred area between social welfare and crime control policies and the ways in which it is managed.

■ *Community: Welfare, Crime and Society*, edited by Gerry Mooney and Sarah Neal. At the heart of this book is an examination of the unique ability of the idea of community to work effectively as shorthand for collective well-being and positive social relations, and as a means of categorising social problems and 'problem populations'. It is this paradox that makes the idea of community a valuable lens for understanding the diverse and complex ways in which social welfare policies and crime control policies collide.

Each book is self-contained and can be read on its own or studied as part of a wide range of courses in universities and colleges. Because these books are integral elements of an Open University course (*Welfare, crime and society*), they are designed as interactive teaching texts to meet the needs of distance learners. The chapters form a planned sequence: each chapter builds on its predecessors. References backwards and forwards to other books and book chapters in the series are highlighted in bold type. Each chapter concludes with a set of suggestions for further reading in relation to its core topics. The chapters are also organised around a number of student-friendly exercises that encourage active learning:

■ *Activities*: highlighted in colour, these are exercises which invite the reader to take an active part in working on the text and are intended to develop understanding and reflective analysis;

■ *Comments*: these provide feedback from the chapter's author(s) on the activities and enable the reader to compare their responses with the thoughts of the author(s).

The production of this book, and the two others that make up the series, draws on the expertise of a wide range of people beyond its editors and authors. Each book reflects the combined efforts of an Open University course team: the 'collective teacher' at the heart of the Open University's educational system. The Open University academics on the *Welfare, crime and society* course team are mainly based in the Department of Social Policy and Criminology in the Faculty of Social Sciences. Each chapter in these books has been through a thorough process of drafting and review to refine both its contents and its teaching approach. This process of development leaves us indebted to the consultant authors, tutor advisers and the course assessor. It also brings together and benefits from a range of other skills and expertise – secretarial staff, editors, designers, audio and video producers, librarians – to translate the ideas into the finished product. All of these activities are held together by the course team manager and course team chairs who ensure that all these component parts fit together successfully. Our thanks to all the contributors to this series.

Sarah Neal and Nicola Yeates, Series Editors

Chapter 1
The search for security

Allan Cochrane and Deborah Talbot

Contents

1   Introduction

The search for security and the threat of insecurity have become central themes in contemporary society. They are reflected in the most intimate aspects of our personal lives as well as being expressed at the largest scales of international events and translated into national and local policy initiatives relating to welfare and crime control.

Activity 1.1

Think about the idea of security – what does it mean to you? To what extent do you feel that an interest in security derives from feeling insecure, and, perhaps, feeling less secure than in the past? Do you think your social position – for example, your gender, your age, your social class, income or wealth, your ethnicity, your nationality – affects your own sense of security?

Comment

While preparing this introductory chapter, we pulled together just a few of the ways in which security seems to be commonly understood or aspired to:

- Emotional security (feeling loved or nurtured by others).

- Financial security (having the financial resources – in property, investments, etc. – to secure one's future).

- Economic security (stable sources of income from work, income support, pensions and so on – sometimes called social security).

- Personal security (feeling safe from threats of violence or incivility).

- Health security (medical and caring support in times of illness).

- Household security (installing locks, alarms, fencing, and so on).

- Housing security (access to adequate and reliable shelter or accommodation).

- Resource security (e.g. access to adequate supplies of water, food and energy).

- National security (protects the nation from internal or external threats).

- Environmental security (managing global warming, pollution and waste).

This list suggests that the notion of security raises some fundamental questions. First, it looks as if each idea of security implies the threat of insecurity, so that insecurity and security are intertwined. We identify certain practices that will make us safe, such as putting locks on our doors or even burglar alarms on our houses, because of the threat of crime. Second, it appears that forms of insecurity differ across time and space. The idea of environmental security – in response to the threat of global warming, pollution and other environmental threats – has seemed more significant in recent years. Sources of security are also located in different spaces. Some sources of security, such as emotional and personal security, are very near to us as individuals; some, such as health or housing security, appear as national problems; others are more international or global. The threat or experience of war, terrorism pursued by states or radical groups, environmental or corporate crimes, the growth of global inequalities, attempts to wipe out populations and races, crises of natural resources: all these seem remote sources of insecurity, but they nonetheless intersect with our everyday lives in troubling and unpredictable ways.

Of course, it is important to add that where we are and who we are influences our experience of security. So, for example, the aspiration to create a 'home owning democracy' as a source of long-term security fits uneasily with the realities of homelessness or even the difficulty that those with low and even middle incomes have in purchasing 'affordable' housing. Moving outside the UK, housing aspirations are likely to be very different. The housing target identified in the UN's Millennium Development Goals is the rather more modest one of achieving a 'significant improvement in the lives of at least 100 million slum dwellers, by 2020' (UN, 2007), which suggests an altogether different set of realities and problems for the global poor.

The aims of this book are to:

- examine the changing ways in which social problems have been interpreted and managed over time

- look at how these changes interact with personal experiences of insecurity and the demand for security

- highlight the powerful ways in which welfare, crime and society are entangled in the search for security and review the ways in which notions of security and insecurity have been mobilised in the development of public policy

- explore the ways in which different sorts of evidence can be used to analyse the development of particular policy initiatives and their impact on a range of social groups

- consider the ways in which evidence is used in the process of policymaking.

In particular, it will consider and look for answers to the following questions:

- Why has security become such an important idea and how does the concept of security link the different domains of social, personal and political life, and especially the worlds of crime control and welfare?

- Why do people and governments invest so much in the pursuit of different forms of security? How might we understand the types of policy and political responses that are generated by the search for security?

- How do we make sense of the changing nature of the relationship between security and insecurity, as expressed in social welfare and crime control policy?

- Why do the measures pursued to provide security often not deliver it – indeed, instead often seem to enhance a sense of insecurity?

In Section 2, we begin by contrasting some contemporary and competing policy perspectives on security, highlighting the uneasy relationships between them. Section 3 then examines how social scientists have attempted to explain the changing relationship between welfare and crime control in contemporary societies. In Section 4, we explore policies and practices aimed at creating a more secure society, before drawing the chapter together in Section 5.

2   Security and public policy

In 2006, John Reid, the British Home Secretary, delivered a speech to Demos, a think tank influential with the government of the time. In this speech, he put forward the argument that the unprecedented threats to security in the UK justified a changed approach to civil liberties and the operation of criminal justice. Reid pointed to what he identified as the destabilising impact of economic change, mass migration and terrorism. He argued that the government needed to rethink its attitude towards migrants, recognising their economic contribution but also the perceived risks to jobs, communities and national security. The range of anti-terror legislation passed and planned alongside the strengthening of European borders were seen as essential to protect the democratic values of the West.

Activity 1.2

Read the following extract from the speech and do the following:

■ Make a list of words used to describe the source of insecurity and the words used to describe what is seen as necessary to provide security.

■ Examine your list of words, concepts or ideas. Do the words used to describe the source of insecurity make you feel afraid? What sorts of policy changes are implied by the conclusions that are drawn?

Extract 1.1

Uncertainty and insecurity is now something that has become a complex woven cloth which spreads across international affairs and defence into domestic affairs and runs from international terrorism and migration right down to the level of your local street and the anti-social behaviour on it and the great social changes taking place there.

...

And I make this point about the requirement for a fundamental understanding of the nature of the struggle in which we are engaged, which will be wide, it will be long, it will be deep, and it will be difficult ... I make it for this reason – because our adversaries in international terrorism are completely unconstrained. The international terrorists of today are ruthless and unconstrained in every direction including in their attempts to misuse our freedoms to undermine our free society. They try to turn to their advantage our society's great strengths in the modern version of what analysts ... used to call asymmetric warfare – identify the strength of your enemy and turn that into a weakness – and in our society, what they want to do is take our society's great strengths, like the free media, ease of access to travel or to goods, and turn them into our weaknesses. They endeavour to drain our morale through the misuse of our freedoms by misrepresenting every mistake or over-reaction as if it is our primary or real purpose. We should not allow ourselves to be seduced by the terrorist who urges to be the quickest to condemn our security forces and police on every occasion and the slowest to understand the problems which they face in tackling a new unconstrained enemy.

Some of them fight for asylum in the United Kingdom, asylum from repressive regimes. Not just for our liberty or the opposite of oppression, but to plan and plot, to establish even more suppressive regimes. Some of them come as students, yet freely express contempt for the intellectual freedoms that have been the bedrock of our scientific advance and academic institutions. Some of them claim to detest usury but fund their plots through fraud, corruption and organised crime.

...

And at a time when a single terrorist could cause irreparable damage on a hitherto unknown scale to our society, ... I find myself in a situation where in dealing with foreign national terrorist suspects we can't always prosecute individuals, due to the difficulties in obtaining sufficiently cogent admissible evidence for a criminal trial. Often we can't deport them, even if they have no proper basis for claiming asylum here, due to concerns about treatment they may receive in their home country as a result of European Court judgements. When considering whether or not they are safe if deported, which I have to do; I am prohibited from considering whether the other 60 million people of this country are safe if they stay here, I am actually prohibited from weighing that in the balance. ...

... I sincerely believe these issues have to be addressed if we are to get maximum protection for the security of our country.

Home Office Press Office, 2006

Comment

So what are the terms used to describe the threats facing us in the UK? One of these is 'international terrorism' – described as 'unconstrained', 'ruthless', with adversaries who want to 'drain our morale', 'misuse our freedoms', funding their 'plots' through 'fraud, corruption and organised crime'. International terrorism is also discussed alongside *and in conjunction with* the effects of migration and antisocial behaviour in our communities. To some extent, Reid also discusses the liberties we enjoy in the UK, and human rights policies aimed at providing safe havens for those persecuted abroad, as if they constitute a threat, preventing the security services from taking effective action. The language used is negative and encourages us to associate our legitimate and palpable fears of terrorism with migration, antisocial behaviour, and our own naive attachment to civil liberties. The implication seems to be that it is necessary to give up some of these liberties and protections so that the population can be protected more effectively.

Would changes along these lines make you feel safer? One paradox, long identified by writers such as Cohen (2002 [1972]), is that in order to justify 'law and order' measures the population needs to feel insecure and threatened. A second is that the apparently ubiquitous existence of security measures, from CCTV (closed-circuit television) to security announcements at train stations, may serve to remind us continually of the threat, paradoxically making us feel more insecure. Some people may also be made more vulnerable by new security measures, because of the increased use by police of a range of powers to stop and search people, which particularly affect those from minority ethnic communities (Home Office, 2005).

Other possible responses to the threats – such as education, initiatives against national and international poverty, moving more effectively against conflict and war – are not explored in the speech.

Activity 1.3

Now read the extract below from a speech delivered by Amartya Sen in 2000, entitled 'Why human security' and ask the same questions of it that we identified for the speech by John Reid.

In this speech Sen expounds the idea of 'human security', which will be examined further in Chapter 5. He draws on a definition introduced by Obuchi Keizo (who at the time was Prime Minister of Japan). For Keizo, human security was about challenging 'all of the menaces that threaten the survival, daily life, and dignity of human beings'.

Extract 1.2

The particular reasons for trying to make a concerted effort [to address issues of human security] precisely at this time are both negative and positive. The negative reasons include the fact that each of these problems have received some set-back in recent years from newly developing dangers and adversities, and these call for specific engagement right now. For example, the prospects of survival have been made less favourable in many parts of the world through problems in public health, including the emergence and spread of particular diseases, such as AIDS, new types of malaria, drug-resistant TB, and so on. Similarly, in the growing persistence and sometimes accentuation of civil wars and associated killings, there is a continuing and worsening threat to survival of civilians caught in the battle of armies and in sectarian genocide or persecution. ...

On the positive side, however, there is an enhanced possibility in the contemporary world to put our efforts and understanding together to achieve a better coordinated resistance to the forces that make human survival so insecure. We live in a world that is not only full of dangers and threats, but also one where the nature of the adversities are better understood, the scientific advances are more firm, and economic and social assets that can counter these menaces are more extensive. Not only do we have more problems to face, we also have more opportunities to deal with them.

... For example, despite the fact that the economic progress of East and South-east Asia had been very rapid for many decades, and notwithstanding the fact that daily lives in the region did improve in many different ways, the danger of a downturn affecting the lives of hundreds of millions also remained firmly present (even if concealed in the euphoria associated with high and seemingly invulnerable growth rates). When the Asian economic crisis came [in 1997], the potential danger – already present – became manifest and fierce, and it ravaged the daily lives of people who had earlier felt falsely secure.

On the other side, however, this experience itself has taught the world many different things which can now be put to use in a concerted promotion of security of daily life. Along with the old slogan of 'growth with equity' we also need a new commitment towards 'downturn with security,' given the fact that occasional downturns are common – possibly inescapable – in market economies. In achieving security under these circumstances, and in trying to guarantee secure daily living in general, we need social and economic provisions (for example, for so-called 'economic safety nets' and the guaranteeing of basic education and health care), but also political participation, especially by the weak and the vulnerable, since their voice is vitally important. This requires the establishment and efficient working of democracies with regular elections and the tolerance of opposition, but also the cultivation of a culture of open public discussion. Democratic participation can directly enhance security through supporting human dignity ... but [it also helps] in securing the continuation of daily lives (despite downturns) and even the security of survival (through the prevention of famines).

Sen, 2000

Comment

Here we can identify more or less the same threats outlined by Reid and some new ones: economic insecurity, conflict and war, genocide and persecution, and disease. There are two key differences in this speech, however: first, the language seems less negative, stressing positive human achievements as well as possible threats; and second, the solutions proposed are the provision of economic safety nets, health care, education and other social goods. Indeed, contrary to Reid's argument, the enhancement of democratic rights is proposed as a precondition for global security.

In essence, then, Extracts 1.1 and 1.2 offer two distinct positions or arguments on a range of fairly similar sets of social problems. Our aim here is not to argue that one is better than the other, but to identify what these positions are. Reid's argument is one commonly associated with 'crime control' – the solution to crime and violence being to increase the scope of criminal law and the powers of the institutions of criminal justice. In Extract 1.2 Sen's argument is a more 'welfarist' one, suggesting that problems of crime and violence need to be placed in the context of poverty and inequality. As a result, Sen stresses the need to improve access to secure jobs, housing, health, as well as to a safety net when things go wrong. Elsewhere, he develops this argument by noting that the relationship between poverty and violence is not a simple one, and highlights the way in which it intersects with issues of identity and culture and the divisions associated with them (see, for example, Sen, 2008). But the importance of challenging poverty and inequality remains a central concern.

These two approaches get to the heart of the content and argument of this book, which is concerned with the ways in which notions of security are expressed in the relationship between crime control and social welfare. They express a central dilemma faced by governments and the wider intellectual and policy community in tackling core problems that underpin the search for security. The book explores the extent to which the crime control vision, expressed by Reid, may be achieving rhetorical and policy dominance over Sen's welfarist perspective in the early twenty-first century. Of course, the story is not so simple. As you will see throughout this book, crime control perspectives may incorporate some welfarist ones, just as welfarist – or care-oriented – ones may incorporate disciplinary measures. Chapter 5 will return to the core contestation of national and human security by looking at the relationship between disease, war and social systems, and how the two perspectives are irreversibly entangled.

So far, therefore, we have identified two differing perspectives and policy solutions proposed to the dilemma of insecurity and the pursuit of security. We will now return to the four questions posed in Section 1 about the ways in which these conflicts and tensions can be understood, and why security has become such a pressing policy concern. We will focus on the relationship between insecurity and security as a core dynamic of the shifts in welfare and crime control policy since the 1980s.

3   Late modernity, insecurity and punitiveness

The view that previously 'secure' Western societies have faced rapid and significant social changes underlies debates about the ways in which public policy has increasingly been directed towards the management of insecurity. These changes have sometimes been summarised in the notion of 'late modernity' – a sense of a fast moving and uncontrollable set of social changes brought about by

> mass migration and tourism, the 'flexibility' of labour, the breakdown of community, the instability of family, the rise of virtual realities and reference points within the media as part of the process of cultural globalisation, the impact of mass consumerism, and the idealisation of individualism, choice and spontaneity.
>
> (Young, 2007, p. 1)

Young (2007) argues that late modern societies have introduced new patterns of inclusion and exclusion, affecting the ways in which people respond to their circumstances. He highlights a tension that is expressed in the ways in which dominant forms of 'cultural inclusion' are accompanied by what he calls 'systematic structural exclusion' (Young 2003, p. 397). By cultural inclusion, Young means the way in which it is increasingly assumed that everyone is treated equally in their relationship to a series of social and economic institutions, including those of education, the media, the criminal justice system, local democracy and consumption. In the promotion of this supposedly 'meritocratic' culture, there is no expectation that any particular group is less worthy of support, respect or access to cultural resources than any other: on the contrary, the expectation is that opportunity is open and available to all.

However, in practice, Young notes, these same institutions also exclude on a selective basis. For example, access to, and success within, education is influenced by class and income, which may be reflected in the ability to move to an expensive catchment area so that one's child can gain access to a good or highly rated school. Similarly, whatever the rhetoric of inclusion (expressed, for example, in the celebration of street fashion sold through retail chains oriented towards young people), consumption depends on access to money or credit. Such forms of inclusion are not the same as equality or equalisation (**Clarke, 2008**). One's treatment within the criminal justice system is also shaped by one's age, gender, class and ethnicity. Hence the cultural aspiration of equality and meritocracy consistently confronts a reality of continued social inequality, undermining the prospect of social justice (see, for example, **Newman and Yeates, 2008**). This is what Young means by 'systematic structural exclusion'.

Young argues that this tension between cultural inclusion and structural exclusion causes resentment, which makes it more likely that poorer people may resort to crime to achieve taken-for-granted social and cultural standards; for example, through the acquisition of consumer goods. At the same time he goes on to suggest that 'lower' middle-class people also experience economic and social insecurity but without the benefits or welfare provision that are available to those out of work. This leaves them feeling resentment towards both directors of large companies who award themselves huge bonuses – the 'fat cats' – and those in receipt of state financial help – the 'welfare scroungers' or 'single mothers' (Young, 2007). The criminality generated by poverty and exclusion is also perceived as an additional threat, while the traditional route to success and monetary gain – hard work – seems to have disappeared. Massive social changes combined with confusion as to status, roles and rewards mean that it is difficult to attain a sense of identity or worth. According to Young, it is this which underlies contemporary insecurities. He uses the term 'ontological insecurity' to describe this confusion – that is, an ongoing and disparate feeling of precariousness in one's daily life and in one's sense of self, a lack of confidence in one's own identity. From this perspective, therefore, the task is to find some way of tying down and directing these anxieties – and one of the means of doing this is to blame, to punish and to find ways of excluding those identified as undeserving, a cause of social problems, the perpetrators of crime and antisocial behaviour. As Young argues:

> just as the relative deprivation and ontological uncertainties of the poor can lead to crime, so perhaps more paradoxically, the deprivation and insecurity of the more wealthy can lead to feelings of punitiveness.
>
> (Young, 2007, p. 36)

Young suggests that these social changes and dislocations have led to society, and policymaking, becoming more punitive. Punitivity (or punitiveness) is a term which means that *systems of punishment have become harsher and that these tough measures have a large degree of popular support.*

Chapter 2 of this book will explore some of the social mechanisms (such as gated communities and sports utility vehicles, or SUVs) used by people to separate themselves from social groups they find threatening or problematic, as well as considering the role of the media in reinforcing forms of insecurity. However, these attitudes are not just expressed culturally, but also find an expression in policy. In the next section we will look at whether and how punitiveness is expressed in crime control and social welfare policy.

4   Policy responses: the shifting boundaries between social welfare and crime control

In contemporary Western societies the division between crime control and welfare is blurred, with the two coming together to produce a complex and sometimes ambiguous policy mix, within which crime control policy substitutes for welfare but may also incorporate welfarist notions of care and protection – see, for example, the discussion in Chapters 3 and 4 of this book, which explores how policies such as child protection, risk assessment, antisocial behaviour and restorative justice have blurred these two distinct institutional fields. The threat and fear of crime, deriving from the social changes we examined in Section 3, has impacted on public and policy attitudes towards welfare and crime control through a process of innovation in law and policy that blurs the boundaries between traditional crime control and welfare fields.

The policy innovations cannot all be characterised as punitive in intent. Garland (2001a), for example, argues that we have shifted to a dual system of policy based around two institutional fields and ideological approaches. He labels the first *punitive segregation* – an increase in control and the utilisation of what he calls 'expressive punishment' – the motivation for justice being retribution or revenge; and he labels the second *preventative partnership*, characterised by a withdrawal of the centralised control of criminal justice in favour of working to control crime through community partnerships and a new emphasis on crime prevention (see also **Hughes, 2009**). The former may be characterised as punitive, the latter as a 'softer' set of innovations aimed at preventing social problems before they emerge. Yet, as you will see in Sections 4.1 and 4.2, the extent of punitiveness may be overestimated in particular policy fields, while strategies aimed at prevention can lead unwittingly to punitiveness.

This is just one of the examples of the complex entanglement between welfare and crime control. It is also possible to identify another broad tendency which can be identified as 'responsibilisation'. This implies that individuals and communities have to take responsibility for their own welfare position, and in policy terms is associated with a series of economic and social incentives and disincentives aimed at reinforcing appropriate behaviour. We will look at some of the implications of this more closely in Section 4.3. A second tendency relates to the expansion of legal regulation (rather than direct intervention) aimed at influencing social and institutional behaviours, and is introduced in Section 4.4.

4.1 A punitive drift?

When faced with issues of security such as crime, governments tend to respond by passing more draconian laws and escalating prison rates. In England and Wales, for example, around 3023 new offences were created between 1997 and 2006, whereas 'only' 500 new offences were created between 1988 and 1997 (Morris, 2006). The prison population in England and Wales increased from 44,719 in 1992 to 80,229 in 2007 and there was also a significant increase in Scotland (from 5357 to 7261) (International Centre for Prison Studies, 2007). It is not just the number of offences and the number incarcerated that have increased. The number of those in prison with serious social or mental health problems is also a cause for concern. Some commentators (see Pratt et al., 2005) suggest that there has been a punitive drift in the policy reaction to crime and the disposal of offenders.

Activity 1.4

Research by Singleton et al. (1998) on over 3000 male and female prisoners found that there was a high correlation between mental health problems and imprisonment. Look at Table 1.1, taken from this research. It indicates the percentage of male and female prisoners (on remand and sentenced) who have been diagnosed as having mental disorders, ranging from antisocial personality disorder to psychosis.

■ What percentage of male sentenced prisoners had two or more mental disorders?

■ What percentage of female sentenced prisoners had no mental disorders?

■ What implications do you think these figures have for understanding why people are in prison?

Table 1.1 Number of mental disorders by prisoner type and sex (shown as %)

Number of disorders	Male remand	Male sentenced	Female remand	Female sentenced
None	5	8	4	10
1	14	20	13	19
2	28	28	22	28
3	32	30	34	24
4	19	12	21	15
5	3	2	6	3
Base	*1250*	*1121*	*187*	*584*

Source: Singleton et al., 1998, p. 24, Table 12.1

Comment

As can be seen from the table, 72 per cent of male sentenced prisoners had two or more mental disorders and only 10 per cent of female sentenced prisoners had no diagnosed mental disorder. The evidence would seem to bear out the view that the prison population could be characterised as 'having problems' rather than 'being problems'. The researchers identified 'risk factors' for mental disorders as including previous experience of a care institution; unemployment; prior offending or being a victim of crime; serious and stressful life events such as sexual abuse, death of a relative, or bullying; ethnicity; social isolation; drinking or drug use. While those in prison had offended or been charged with an offence (they were 'on remand'), these data suggest that prison might not be the most effective way of dealing with the cause of their offending.

Figure 1.1
Inside a prison

The close interrelationship between social marginalisation and being the target of a punitive response by government is even more striking in the USA. Wacquant (2001, 2005), for example, has identified a close association between the perceived dangerousness of African American males and the rise and composition of the prison population in the USA. The prison has been extended into what he calls 'a single *carceral continuum* which entraps a redundant population of younger black men (and increasingly women) in the urban ghettoes as well as the formal prisons' (Wacquant, 2002, pp. 52–3). The USA has a prison population of over 2 million, of whom 70 per cent are black or Latino while two thirds of African American men in their twenties living in the north-eastern cities of the USA are either in prison, on probation or on parole (Peck, 2003, p. 226; Young, 1999, p. 18). This level of imprisonment and other forms of containment, says Wacquant, has less to do with crime rates – which fell slightly during the period of prison expansion dating from 1973 – and more to do with changing official attitudes towards poverty and the fear of disorderliness:

What changed during the intervening decades, then, is not the frequency and character of criminal activity but the *attitude of*

the society and the responses of the authorities toward street delinquency
and its principal source, urban poverty concentrated in the big cities.
... The prison has been called upon to contain the disorders generated
by the rising tide of dispossessed families, street derelicts, unemployed
and alienated youths, and the desperation and violence that have
accumulated and intensified in the segregated urban core of the
metropolis as the 'safety net' of the US semi-welfare state was torn,
and desocialized wage-labour in the low-wage service sectors was
made the normal horizon of work for deskilled fractions of the
working class.

(Wacquant, 2005, p. 15)

Wacquant argues that the prison and other forms of behaviour
management such as electronic tagging and probation have less to do
with rising crime rates and are more concerned with managing *disorder* –
a vague and slippery term that can express a wide range of behaviours,
not necessarily directly criminal. This is also apparent in some of the
arguments of the so-called 'broken windows thesis' (Wilson and Kelling,
1982), which has been enthusiastically embraced by policymakers in the
USA and the UK. It suggests that small social infractions ranging from
the physical decay of neighbourhoods, littering, begging, drunkenness,
noise and the congregation of young people may ultimately encourage
criminality by making communities afraid of intervening in unwanted
behaviour, thereby creating a psychological space for rule breaking. As
well as influencing policing strategies across Europe and North America,
this understanding has also encouraged the development of strategies
aimed at controlling antisocial behaviour, like those in the UK explored
further in Chapter 4.

The USA has an exceptionally high rate of imprisonment for a
democratic country, which also disproportionately affects particular
social groups, especially African Americans and Latinos. As a result, the
US system of punishment has been summed up in the concept of *mass
imprisonment* (Garland, 2001b). By contrast, while actual prison rates in
the UK have nearly doubled since 1992, they remain substantially lower
than in the USA. In the UK in 2007, the imprisonment rate was below
150 per 100,000 of the population while in the USA, in 2006, it
amounted to 751 per 100,000 of the population (International Centre for
Prison Studies, 2007). In the UK (and other European countries), the
policy context remains rather different, with a greater emphasis on other
forms social intervention, which do not necessarily lead to prison.

The notion of a punitive drift seems to accord with some aspects of the
changes that we have identified but its significance has also been
questioned. Matthews (2005), for example, argues that, on the one
hand, crime control policies have always been punitive, so there is

nothing new in what we are witnessing; on the other, it may simply be a case that there are punitive tendencies in some, but not all, countries or that countries may have a different mix of punitive policies and more welfarist ones. This insight highlights the importance of examining critically the evidence that is said to support the claims of a widespread drift towards punitiveness, rather than simply accepting it as a universal trend.

4.2 Prevention and risk management

So far, we have touched upon changes within the traditional justice system – such as the criminal law, prisons and policing. Garland (2001a), however, also identifies the emergence of a parallel sector, namely 'preventative partnership'. Proponents of the preventative approach argue that it is not punitive because it is not primarily aimed at punishing individuals but simply at altering the physical and social environment so as to influence behaviours. Prevention involves the mobilisation of a range of different techniques to reduce opportunities for crime to occur. One of these techniques involves the placing of physical barriers between the opportunistic criminal and the object of crime – this is known as 'situational crime prevention'. You may have noticed CCTV cameras in your neighbourhood, a major preventative technique aiming to act as a deterrent. You may also have noticed that new residential blocks no longer have dark and invisible enclosures – all new building aims in various ways to 'design out crime'. This reflects the impact of UK-wide schemes such as 'secured by design', which is run through the Association of Chief Police Officers (ACPO). Before developers are granted planning permission for new housing they are required to consult local police who assess all new developments to ensure that they incorporate crime prevention techniques in their design; for example, by reducing multi-access and exit points and increasing the visibility of public areas to residents to encourage 'natural surveillance'.

In addition, it has become common for government to try to involve 'communities' in crime prevention, through schemes ranging from Neighbourhood Watch to Safer Neighbourhood Teams and Crime and Disorder Prevention or Community Safety Partnerships (**Hughes, 2009**). In these 'partnerships', various actors, such as the council, the police, business people, and residents amongst others in the 'community', are brought together with the aim of finding ways of managing local populations to reduce the incidence of crime. This is known as 'social crime prevention'.

Figure 1.2
The search for security:
cameras promise
neighbourhood
security; speaking into
an entry phone to gain
access to a block of flats;
personal security –
chains and locks on a
front door

Another example of this approach can be seen in the BIDs (Business
Improvement Districts) programmes, which originated in New York, but
have spread to other cities in the USA, to the UK and through Europe.
They provide ways of mobilising commercial interests to maintain and
protect the areas within which their businesses are located, through
'soft' interventions – for example, street cleaning, the provision of street
furniture and decoration. They also include potentially 'harder' forms of
intervention, such as the use of neighbourhood patrols, to deal with
problematic behaviour. They are funded through a voluntary system of
taxation on the owners of property and businesses – outside the
traditional forms of public finance – and in some cases (e.g. in Central
Manhattan) have been in a position to invest in infrastructural and
other commercial development (Zukin, 1995, pp. 33–8; 66–7). Like many
regeneration initiatives, they have tended to prioritise commercial
development over community development and have sometimes created
conflicts over who and what our cities and public spaces are for, even if
they have sometimes also generated spaces that are attractive to local
residents (Zukin, 1995, pp. 36–7).

However, the notion of prevention is one that stretches across the arena
of social policy, drawing in a wide range of agencies. So, for example, the
emphasis on safeguarding children – reflected among other places in the
framework for England and Wales, *Every Child Matters* (DfES, 2003) and
in the framework for Scotland, *Getting it Right for Every Child* (Scottish
Executive, 2005) – places great stress on providing support for children
and young people and their families in order to prevent the emergence
of social problems later in life. These policies are discussed further in
Chapter 3. The expectation is that agencies from social services to
police, health service to schools, and professionals from social workers

to police officers, doctors and nurses to schoolteachers, will all work together to ensure that children and young people will be able to develop their potential in safety and security.

Underpinning many of these new preventative strategies are professional strategies that aim to identify risk factors that might emerge later as problematic or criminal behaviours. For example, the research by Singleton et al. (1998), considered in Activity 1.4 in the previous section, aimed to demonstrate the risk factors that had subsequently led to offending by those in the prison population. This research suggested that the prison population consisted of people with personal and social problems that might account for their behaviour, and who might have benefited from earlier social – welfarist – intervention. With children and young people, the identification and assessment of risk can lead to a variety of interventions that span the welfare/crime control continuum. These include:

■ positive forms of encouragement and support; for example, schemes that are intended to help children at school or to provide early years learning

■ monitoring of children at risk, which may lead to their removal from the home or to therapeutic involvement

■ attempts to change behaviour through exhortation; for example, campaigns on sexual health and even healthy eating

■ behaviour management through, for example, youth offending teams, Community Orders, Anti-social Behaviour Orders (ASBOs), or the use of preventative detention and imprisonment (these issues are further discussed in Chapters 3 and 4).

What is interesting about these interventions are the ways in which they interlock and interconnect in practice, so that the failure of even the most apparently supportive of interventions can lead towards more punitive and disciplinary responses.

Activity 1.5

Barron (2007) conducted qualitative research amongst young female offenders (most of whom were from Canadian Aboriginal peoples) in three youth custody centres in Canada to explore the impact of risk assessment tools and strategies on the culture of these institutions. The following extract looks at how young women's sexual behaviour was identified as risky, which led to increased sensitivity about all physical contact between the young women. Read the extract, and think about the various ways in which risk assessment techniques helped define sexual behaviour amongst the young women as risky. What impact do you think the heightened emphasis on security and risk management had on the young women's welfare?

Extract 1.3

The effect of risk thinking combined with heterosexism is that some aggressive girls are managed in the youth detention centre as sexual deviants. There is a sense by staff that the contact between the girls is 'unwelcomed' and is making some girls feel uncomfortable. One of the staff indicated that there are informal discussions on the unit that, if the behaviour persists, the staff will have to separate the furniture to prevent inappropriate touching: this is the arrangement in the sex offender unit. ... Some of the rules to control girls' behaviour do not exist on the boys' unit. As Kristine [one of the young women] states, to prevent girls from having a relationship 'we have a no-touching rule. ... And that's why we can't share rooms unless it's a full dorm and then they'll put sisters together first.' One of the teachers reacts in frustration about this rule: 'if one of the girls is gay then you need to deal with that ... not as abnormal but as part of life. That doesn't mean you create a policy where they can never be in the same room together.' Stemming from risk logics, the 'risk' of same sex experimentation developing is managed by taking away the opportunity for any type of physical contact between girls.

Risk strategies for girls in the institution preclude sexual experimentation. Although one staff comments that some girls sexually 'prey' on others, none of the girls report being sexually coerced or experiencing unwanted touching by other girls. Kristine explains: 'It is mostly the older girls hooking up. The younger ones aren't involved ... but the younger girls will probably start doing it too when they get older.' It seems, therefore, that sexual contact coincides with maturity and development rather than being the indicator of a predatory relationship. The girls are at an age of sexual exploration and curiosity but they are trapped in an environment that does not allow developmental engagement. As one of the teachers explains:

> The girls don't get their own clothes, they're not allowed to touch each other or do each other's hair unless they ask permission, they're not allowed to wear make-up. ... They're not allowed to talk to the boys, they're not even supposed to look at them so how normal is that?

Barron, 2007, pp. 71–2

Comment

Barron argues that the use of risk assessment techniques, which identified sexual behaviour amongst young people as problematic, led to forms of intervention that negatively affected the welfare of the young people involved. A core part of their development (from sexual development to physical affection) was undermined. Behaviour that would not be so visible or policed in society was highly regulated in the prison environment, because of the heightened fears and anxiety generated by the need to assess 'riskiness'. Conflicts over the care and control of young people are discussed more fully in Chapter 3.

4.3 Making up responsible populations

In the previous section we looked at how particular partnerships have been developed in order to encourage the involvement of communities in the work of crime control and the resolution of social problems. In this way, with the help of government, communities were made 'responsible' for their own welfare (see also **Mooney and Neal, 2009**). A similar process works in other ways through the welfare and crime control systems, making individuals responsible for their own welfare and systems of protection, through governance of their behaviour, rather than top-down authority (**Clarke, 2008**). The 'law-abiding' citizen as well as the 'criminal' or potential criminal are both affected by attempts to manage insecurity.

Rose (2000) identifies a strategy of responsibilisation aimed at each of these groups. Responsibilisation is the process by which individuals are increasingly expected to be responsible for managing their own well-being – as consumers, as 'prudential' financial managers of their lives, as enterprising selves in the workplace or labour market, and as members of communities, seeing to economic, ethical and security interests (Rose, 1999).

In terms of the 'law-abiding' citizen, responsibilisation strategies are mobilised through a range of incentives and disincentives to behave, many of them economic and more narrowly commercial. The need to access credit, for example, to purchase goods, is one means by which our culture facilitates self-improvement and freedom – in other words, a civilised life. We might consider here the effort and passion that goes into buying the right clothes, a good house, a designer kitchen – that is, all the accoutrements that speak of status and success. In order to access credit, or a mortgage, however, it is necessary to maintain a good credit history. Having a good credit history is achieved through being an identifiable person (through having a passport, a driving license or a bank or credit card), through having already accessed credit and maintained that debt efficiently. Such requirements make it necessary to think twice before putting our jobs in jeopardy or engaging in behaviours that might make us a 'bad risk'. Hence the culture of consumption may also have an important (self-)disciplinary aspect.

Figure 1.3
A designer kitchen

The privatisation of social welfare has further encouraged this process of responsibilisation. In this context, social policy is reinterpreted as being about finding ways of 'enabling' or 'empowering' individuals or communities to take on responsibility for their own lives, supporting them in finding work, in bringing up children, in developing appropriate skills, in saving for pensions, in purchasing houses, rather than providing services or – except for those facing the greatest challenges – providing financial maintenance directly to them. So, for example, in the health sphere, **Clarke (2008, Section 4)** identifies how chronically ill people are encouraged to manage their own medication, while campaigns against smoking and obesity also make clear the extent to which people are increasingly deemed responsible for their own ill health.

Activity 1.6

There has been a significant shift in the tenure of housing since the early 1950s. Council or social housing has declined, while home ownership has dramatically increased (to around 70 per cent from

32 per cent in 1953). By late 2007, prices of a UK home had increased to six times the average wage. In what way do you think the British housing market influences behaviour and culture – your own or that of other people? How might this illustrate the responsibilisation thesis as it affects ordinary citizens?

Comment

We identified some of the possible behavioural and cultural impacts of the contemporary housing market, as follows:

■ a need to maintain credit history in order to be able to obtain a mortgage

■ the pressure to work harder and longer as a result of being tied to high levels of debt

■ fear and insecurity about prospects of interest rate rises

■ a concern that houses should increase in value – leading to preoccupation with issues that affect house prices, such as crime, noise, the nature of the area, security, or issues such as decorating in a 'neutral' fashion, all of which are reflected in and reinforced by a series of popular media representations (including a variety of television programmes focused on the purchase, sale or development of houses).

You may have thought of others.

The dominance of home ownership as the favoured model of housing tenure is a persuasive example of the process of responsibilisation, not least because it has been underpinned by an active process of privatisation as council houses have been sold and investment in social housing significantly constrained. Risk has been transferred to home owners, with not only the promise of wealth accumulation as house prices rise, but also the threat of insecurity associated with a possible crash in the housing market. While home ownership was seen in the 1980s as representing freedom and choice – a shift away from the conformity of renting a council house with all the rules and regulations that implied – in many ways it has simply encouraged a different kind of conformity for those bearing the risks and responsibilities of ownership. The pressure to keep the neighbourhood free of crime and disorderliness in order to maintain the value of a house may also help to support the tendency towards punitiveness or vindictiveness identified by Young (2007). Chapter 2 will explore this issue further through the example of gated communities.

Rose also identifies strategies of control aimed at the excluded – the 'welfare dependent' and the 'underclass', as it is disparagingly known (see also **Mooney, 2008**). These, he argues, are seen as 'failed citizens' who must be contained or confined. In Sections 4.1 and 4.2, you saw how this can result in various criminal justice interventions ranging from Anti-Social Behaviour Orders (ASBOs) to prison. However, responsibilising strategies are also targeted on these sections of society with the aim of 'integrating' them; for example through involvement in paid employment.

In this context, paid work has been seen by British governments since the early 1980s as the key means by which the 'underclass' and the socially excluded can break out of the unhealthy and socially unproductive effects of 'welfare dependency' (**Widdowson, 2008**). This reliance on state benefits has been understood by some policy commentators such as Murray (1996) to mean long-term dependence on social security benefits, often over several generations in a family. This is said to give rise to both financial and moral impoverishment and generate wider social 'risks' (see Section 4.2). Various strategies have been developed in a range of countries, including the UK, the USA and Australia, which have aimed to persuade, through incentives and coercion, those in receipt of welfare benefits, including single parents, to take what are often low-income jobs. The benefits of paid work are seen to extend beyond simple financial independence, since the advantages of work are also seen to include self-respect or worth, sustaining families and personal discipline. As Tony Blair (who was then Prime Minister of the UK) argued, when launching the self-employment option of the New Deal for Young People in Dundee in July 1998, 'There are real social and personal benefits in getting people off welfare and into work. Giving people a sense of worth, and helping unemployed people acquire the skills they need to find employment is a moral responsibility' (The Scottish Government, 1998).

The policy implications of welfare-to-work initiatives – as Peck (2001) notes – can be both enabling and punitive/disciplinary. In the UK they have been associated with approaches which emphasise the availability of skills training and the provision of personal advisers helping to place the unemployed in jobs. They were accompanied by the introduction of a minimum wage and the availability of forms of tax credit for those in low-paid jobs. Similarly, the extension of early years education and childcare is intended not only to provide targeted support to vulnerable children but also to ensure that mothers, particularly lone parents, are able to enter the labour market. Legislation ensures that it is no longer possible for employers in the UK and other European countries to discriminate on grounds of disability. However, for those who are deemed not to have taken the opportunities presented to them, rights to certain benefits are increasingly restricted, and possibly removed. Even those in receipt of benefits based on particular disabilities find themselves increasingly challenged to provide medical evidence on an ongoing basis. In other words, for those who do not accept the responsibilities placed on them, disciplinary action of one sort or another is the default option.

In this context, it is important to ask whether work can lead to a sense of self-worth. In 2007, the minimum wage was £5.35 for those over 22, £4.45 for 18 to 21-year-olds, and £3.30 for 16 to 17-year-olds, which is not the means by which any of the indices of financial security – owning a home or even being able to pay for what our society considers to be necessities, such as food, clothing, paying bills – can be achieved. The work is likely to be dull, repetitive, and lacking the features that would provide personal satisfaction (**Widdowson, 2008**). In other words, the breakdown of the implicit 'bargain' of the post-1945 settlement, namely that the majority would undertake ordinary work that might be oppressive and boring but was well enough paid to buy time for leisure and family, has not yet been replaced by one in which everyone is able to realise their potential (Young, 2007). The impact of responsibilisation strategies is discussed further in Chapters 2 and 3.

4.4 Legal regulation and conduct

It has become common for journalists and politicians to argue that we live in an over-regulated society, full of bureaucracy and 'red tape'. This has been identified by social scientists such Habermas (1989) as 'juridification'. Broadly, juridification means the increased reach of law and regulation in social life, to the extent that they affect the everyday ways in which we interact with each other in society.

There are significant tensions within this process, whose outcomes are sometimes uncertain. So, for example, the extent to which schools are restricted in their ability to make independent decisions about learning or behavioural control may be seen to limit their ability to develop effective teaching strategies. The extent to which government has moved towards a conception of itself as 'manager', setting targets for the delivery of pre-agreed strategies to regulate the free market at the margins, may represent a significant narrowing of political action and democratic accountability (Bradley and Walters, 2002). However, for young people at risk of exclusion from education, the possibility of appeal and clear courses of redress may be positive. And, as Chapter 4 will illustrate, juridification also means that the law has increasingly framed protection for minority ethnic groups against discrimination, crime and violence, while human rights and international law have sought to provide basic protections and security against war and disease for civilians, as we will examine in Chapter 5. In these examples, because politics or morality have been seen as inadequate protectors of the welfare of minorities or civilians in general, systems of formal rights or protections are demanded. The law has therefore become a core mediator of welfare and protection, with both positive and negative consequences (see, for example, **Newman and Yeates, 2008**).

Activity 1.7

The following extract is from qualitative research conducted by one of the chapter authors on the development of the night-time economy in an area of London. It discusses the licensing authority's perceptions that its power to control the growth of the night-time economy and later licensing (i.e. outside the agreed normal hours) was constrained by law. Previously, councils could reject later licensing on political or moral grounds. With changes in government policy aimed at encouraging the night-time economy, they had to adhere more closely to legal frameworks and transparent decision making.

Read the extract and think about how licensing regulation influenced each of the following group's ability to exercise power:

- nightclub owners/licensees
- council officers
- residents.

Extract 1.4

The drive towards consistency, transparency and evidence-based decision making was underlined by the perceived threat by practically all officers and councillors interviewed of appeal to the courts. According to the Borough Solicitor, for example, although many premises accepted that the Committee's decision was final, larger operators commonly resorted to appeal, revealing a defect in the process of objections whereby councillors had to take into account the views of residents and other bodies:

> Sometimes, they accept that [the decision]. Others, like the Palace [a large nightclub], say no, we're appealing. This is an unreasonable decision you've come to. It goes to the magistrates' court. They don't look at the Committee's decision. You have the problem then that all the objectors that came along to the council meeting are often reluctant to take the day off work or whatever to come along to a court hearing and give that same evidence, and places like the Palace, they throw a lot of money in it. It's big business to them.

They do surveys, and people stand outside and monitor the traffic and the noise, and say, well, at this time there's 500 cars go by every twenty minutes so it doesn't make any difference, and people come out, there's never any trouble. It's difficult for the Council to actually fight that. They do the best they can. Members have actually gone to court and say 'I objected at the time, and this is the reason why – I had all these people coming to me and complaining'.

The fear of legal challenge, therefore, was perceived to have stymied the Council's ability to control the activities of night-time business, particularly those able to access legal representation.

Talbot, 2007, pp. 95–6

Comment

It is arguable here that the powers of nightclub operators were enhanced by the changes taking place in licensing regulation, while those of the council and residents to protect themselves against noise and nuisance were diminished. This might be viewed as negative in so far as it undermined 'local democracy' and therefore the welfare of residents. However, the research also found that without legal consistency, councils, along with police and magistrates, tended to make subjective and prejudicial judgements about licensees on grounds of 'race', gender, or the nature of the business. It could therefore be argued that the welfare of small businesses – who often struggle to maintain themselves – was enhanced by these changes towards legal consistency. However, when everyone in this process is construed as a legal subject with irreconcilable interests, as is the case with local licensing decisions, it raises questions about whether the law can create an effective mechanism for deciding what is best for communities as a whole.

Can you think of any other examples of expansion of legal regulation? You might think here of legislation around noise and nuisance, controls over cars and parking, parenting classes (examined further in Chapter 3), or antisocial behaviour (discussed in Chapter 4). What do you think the benefits and drawbacks of these legal changes might be for different social groups?

5   Review

In this chapter we have been concerned to highlight some of the important questions that arise from looking at the ways in which security and insecurity interrelate with core concerns of welfare and crime control policy. We have examined some of the key perspectives, which describe how the interrelationships between welfare and crime control concerns have altered. The remaining chapters will explore how these trends have emerged and developed in four key areas, and how strategies aimed at producing security can often lead to greater insecurity, not less.

In Chapter 2, Yvonne Jewkes explores, through the examples of gated communities and the growing use of sports utility vehicles (SUVs), how the concepts of prevention and responsibilisation (including the role of the media) help explain the ways in which individuals seek to manage their own protection. In Chapter 3 Jane McCarthy looks at the complex ways in which families provide a site for a range of interventions, ranging from those aimed at responsibilisation and prevention to more punitive strategies. In Chapter 4, John Muncie and Ross Fergusson examine the relationship between juridification and punitiveness, using the examples of Anti-Social Behaviour Orders (ASBOs), hate crime and restorative justice. In Chapter 5, we return to some of the core dilemmas of this book, the entanglement of crime control and welfare as exemplified by the idea of security, in a global context, with the help of case studies focused on war, health and disease.

Throughout this chapter, we have used different kinds of evidence. In Activities 1.2 and 1.3, in Section 2, we provided extracts from two speeches as exemplars of thinking around the concept of security. In Activity 1.4, we used statistics to look at mental disorders amongst prisoners. In Activities 1.5 and 1.7, we looked at extracts from qualitative case studies. In the following chapters, the book systematically considers the ways in which evidence may be used and interpreted to help answer the questions identified in Section 1. Chapter 2 explores how qualitative case studies can be interpreted, Chapter 3 focuses on the analysis of evidence drawn from documentary texts, Chapter 4 examines the use of crime statistics, and Chapter 5 looks at how evidence may be incorporated into the policy process. The final chapter reviews the arguments of the book, returning to each of the questions raised in Section 1 of this chapter and reflecting on the ways in which evidence has been used to answer them.

Further reading

The Vertigo of Late Modernity (2007, Sage) by Jock Young (to which you have already been introduced in this chapter) provides a helpful way into debates about the relationship between social change and changes in public policy, particularly in its reflections on the rise of punitiveness. David Garland's *The Culture of Control: Crime and Order in Contemporary Society* (2001, Oxford University Press), and which has also been referred to in the chapter, is another book that explores the relationships between social change and the maintenance of social order, highlighting the ways in which crime control and social policy are closely entangled. *Criminology and Social Policy* (2007, Sage) by Paul Knepper is a student-oriented text which explicitly sets out to highlight the importance of criminological perspectives in understanding key areas of social policy, but also to show the importance of social policy to the concerns of criminology. If you wish to pursue issues of social justice further in the context of issues raised in this book, then *Social Justice: Welfare, Crime and Society* (2008, Open University Press/The Open University), edited by Janet Newman and Nicola Yeates, is a helpful companion volume, and issues relating to community are pursued further in *Community: Welfare, Crime and Society* (2009, Open University Press/The Open University), edited by Gerry Mooney and Sarah Neal.

References

Barron, C. (2007) 'A paradigm of exclusion: the impact of the risk society on female young offenders' in Law Commission of Canada (ed.) *Risk and Trust: Including or Excluding Citizens*, Black Point, NS, Fernwood.

Bradley, T. and Walters, R. (2002) 'The managerialisation of crime prevention and community safety: the New Zealand experience' in Hughes, G., McLaughlin, E. and Muncie, J. (eds) *Crime Prevention and Community Safety: New Directions*, London, Sage.

Clarke, J. (2008) 'Looking for social justice: welfare states and beyond' in Newman and Yeates (eds) (2008).

Cohen, S. (2002 [1972]) *Folk Devils and Moral Panics* (3rd edn), London, Routledge.

Department for Education and Skills (DfES)(2003) *Every Child Matters*, London, The Stationery Office; also available online at http://publications. everychildmatters.gov.uk/default.aspx?PageFunction=productdetails&PageMode= publications&ProductId=CM5860& (Accessed 14 December 2007).

Garland, D. (2001a) *The Culture of Control: Crime and Order in Contemporary Society*, Oxford, Oxford University Press.

Garland, D. (ed.) (2001b) *Mass Imprisonment: Social Causes and Consequences*, London, Sage.

Habermas, J. (1989) *A Theory of Communicative Action*, vol. 2, Cambridge, Cambridge University Press.

Home Office (2005) *Statistics on Race and the Criminal Justice System 2005*, London, Home Office, also available online at http://www.homeoffice.gov.uk/rds/pdfs06/s95race05.pdf (Accessed 17 December 2007).

Home Office Press Office (2006) 'Security, freedom and the protection of our values: a speech by the Home Secretary to Demos on 9 August 2006' [online], http://press.homeoffice.gov.uk/Speeches/sp-hs-DEMOS-090806?version=1 (Accessed 13 December 2007).

Hughes, G. (2009) 'Community safety and the governance of "problem" populations' in Mooney, G. and Neal, S. (eds) *Community: Welfare, Crime and Society,* **Maidenhead, Open University Press/Milton Keynes, The Open University.**

International Centre for Prison Studies (2007) 'World prison brief' [online], http://www.kcl.ac.uk/depsta/rel/icps/worldbrief/world_brief.html (Accessed 14 December 2007).

Matthews, R. (2005) 'The myth of punitiveness', *Theoretical Criminology*, vol. 9, no. 2, pp. 175–201.

Mooney, G. (2008) '"Problem" populations, "problem" places' in Newman and Yeates (eds) (2008).

Mooney, G. and Neal, S. (eds) (2009) *Community: Welfare, Crime and Society,* **Maidenhead, Open University Press/Milton Keynes, The Open University.**

Morris, N. (2006) 'Blair's "frenzied law making": a new offence for every day spent in office', *The Independent*, 16 August [online], http://news.independent.co.uk/uk/politics/article1219484.ece (Accessed 14 December 2007).

Murray, C. (1996) *Charles Murray and the Underclass: The Developing Debate*, London, IEA Health and Welfare Unit.

Newman, J. and Yeates, N. (eds) (2008) *Social Justice: Welfare, Crime and Society,* **Maidenhead, Open University Press/Milton Keynes, The Open University.**

Peck, J. (2001) *Workfare States*, New York, NY, The Guilford Press.

Peck, J. (2003) 'Geography and public policy: mapping the penal state', *Progress in Human Geography*, vol. 27, no. 2, pp. 222–32.

Pratt, J., Brown, D., Brown, M., Hallsworth, S. and Morrison, W. (eds) (2005) *The New Punitiveness: Trends, Theories and Perspectives*, Uffculme, Willan Publishing.

Rose, N. (1999) *Powers of Freedom: Reframing Political Thought*, Cambridge, Cambridge University Press.

Rose, N. (2000) 'Government and control', *British Journal of Criminology*, vol. 40, pp. 321–9.

Scottish Executive (2005) *Getting It Right For Every Child: Proposals for Action*, Edinburgh, Scottish Executive; also available online at http://childpolicyinfo.childreninscotland.org.uk/index/news-app?story=3841 (Accessed 27 October 2007).

The Scottish Government (1998) 'The Prime Minister the Rt Hon Tony Blair MP – speech to launch self-employment option of New Deal for Young People – Dundee', news release 1457/98, 17 July [online], http://www.scotland.gov.uk/News/Releases/1998/07/59a505bc-5cf1-4e46-9296-1c496ec69a28 (Accessed 17 December 2007).

Sen, A. (2000) Why human security', text of presentation at the International Symposium on Human Security, Tokyo, 28 July; also available online at http://www.humansecurity-chs.org/activities/outreach/Sen2000.html (Accessed 13 December 2007).

Sen, A. (2008) 'Poverty, war and peace', *The Little Magazine*, vol. 7, nos 3–4, pp. 6–16.

Singleton, N., Meltzer, H. and Gatward, R. (1998) *Psychiatric Morbidity Among Prisoners: Summary Report*, London, Department of Health; also available online at http://www.dh.gov.uk/en/Publicationsandstatistics/Publications/PublicationsStatistics/DH_4007132 (Accessed 17 December 2007).

Talbot, D. (2007) *Regulating the Night: Race, Culture and Exclusion in the Making of the Night-time Economy*, Aldershot, Ashgate.

United Nations (UN) (2007) 'UN Millennium Development Goals' [online], http://www.un.org/millenniumgoals/index.html (Accessed 13 December 2007).

Wacquant, L. (2001) 'Deadly symbiosis: when ghetto and prison meet and mesh' in Garland, D. (ed.) *Mass Imprisonment: Social Causes and Consequences*, London, Sage.

Wacquant, L. (2002) 'From slavery to mass incarceration: rethinking the "race question" in the US', *New Left Review*, vol. 13, pp. 41–60.

Wacquant, L. (2005) 'The great penal leap backward: incarceration in America from Nixon and Clinton' in Pratt, J., Brown, D., Brown, M., Hallsworth, S. and Morrison, W. (eds) (2005) *The New Punitiveness: Trends, Theories and Perspectives*, Uffculme, Willan Publishing.

Widdowson, B. (2008) 'Well-being, harm and work' in Newman and Yeates (eds) (2008).

Wilson, J.Q. and Kelling, G.L. (1982) 'Broken windows: the police and neighbourhood safety', *The Atlantic Monthly*, vol. 249, no. 3, pp. 29–38.

Young, J. (1999) *The Exclusive Society: Social Exclusion, Crime and Difference in Late Modernity*, London, Sage.

Young, J. (2003) 'Merton with energy, Katz with structure: the sociology of vindictiveness and the criminology of transgression', *Theoretical Criminology*, vol. 7, no. 3, pp. 388–414.

Young, J. (2007) *The Vertigo of Late Modernity*, London, Sage.

Zukin, S. (1995) *The Cultures of Cities*, Oxford, Blackwell.

Chapter 2
Insecurity, fear and social retreat

Yvonne Jewkes

Contents

1   Introduction

As you saw in Chapter 1, feelings of security and insecurity take many and varied forms in different times and places. In part this reflects the direct, first-hand experience of people. But the question of whether fear and insecurity are born out of such experiences, or are created, circulated and exacerbated by external forces such as the media in a manner out of proportion to the actual threat, has long been the subject of debate among social scientists. The purpose of this chapter is to explore how social fears are generated, the strategies that people employ to cope with those fears, and the unintended consequences for people as they search for security.

The aims of this chapter are to:

■ further explore the ambiguities and paradoxes inherent in notions of security and insecurity

■ investigate the role of the media and other actors in fostering public fears and anxieties about crime and 'problem' populations and in encouraging strategies of responsibilisation

■ explore the extent to which and ways in which forms of social retreat represent a response to increased fear and insecurity

■ consider the nature and value of qualitative research in helping us to review issues concerning the relationship between insecurity and social retreat.

The chapter first discusses, in Section 2, the role of the media in generating and perpetuating anxieties about crime. In Section 3, it then uses two case studies to consider some of the strategies adopted by people in order to make themselves feel more secure. The first is the phenomenon of gated communities – private sector housing developments that, through the use of gates, barriers and security guards, seek to shield themselves from possible sources of danger. The second case study examines the increased popularity of sports utility vehicles (SUVs), 'four-by-four' or 'off-road' vehicles originally designed for hard-wearing country environments but which have become common in urban areas. The chapter will examine these two cases as forms of 'social retreat' in which people seek to protect themselves against sources of fear, and as examples of 'responsibilisation' in which individuals take private responsibility for their own security. The case studies are used to explore the ways in which social welfare and crime control have become increasingly entangled.

2 The role of the media in generating public insecurities

We start with a discussion of the role of the media in creating and perpetuating public anxieties about crime because it has become increasingly commonplace to view the media as one of the main drivers of public insecurity. In a 1995 MORI poll, 66 per cent of people interviewed said they got their information from television and 33 per cent claimed their fears about crime were increased by news and documentary coverage of crime. But to what extent can the blame for our anxieties justifiably be laid at the doors of the news industry? Certainly it is frequently argued (by politicians, scholars and even by some sections of the media themselves) that news organisations create a false picture of the problem of crime, exaggerating certain categories of offending, such as random and violent attacks by strangers, and ignoring or underplaying other types, such as the crimes of governments and powerful organisations, or 'domestic' crimes within the family. This can result in a distortion of public perceptions about crime, with greatest levels of fear attached to crimes which, statistically, are least likely to affect them. It has been noted that fear of crime often exceeds the actual risk of personal harm. For example, successive British Crime Surveys, which measure experiences of crime among adults aged 16 and over in England and Wales, have reported that 'worry about crime' is frequently highest at times when recorded crimes are falling (Kershaw et al., 2000). Skewed media representations may help to explain why fear of crime is disproportionately felt in the relatively comfortable, low-crime areas of 'middle England' (Girling et al., 2000).

The reasons for the media's preoccupation with serious, random offences of a sexual and/or violent nature may be largely pragmatic and economic. They are, after all, in the business of selling newspapers and gaining audience ratings, and it is the crimes that are statistically least common that are most 'newsworthy' (Jewkes, 2004). However, at the same time as giving extensive and frequently sensationalised treatment to offences that are both very serious and unlikely to happen to most of us, the popular media tend also to promote a nostalgic view that 'things aren't what they used to be' via stories about mundane crime, antisocial behaviour and declining moral values, particularly among certain groups, such as young people or other 'problem populations' (**Mooney, 2008**).

The media images of such 'risky' or dangerous groups of people who are held to be responsible for random violence and antisocial behaviour (see Chapter 4) might reasonably be said to lead to disproportionate feelings of insecurity in the population at large. Research published by the Institute for Public Policy Research (Margo and Dixon, 2006) concludes that Britain is in danger of becoming a nation frightened of its young people. One of its findings is that British adults are less likely than those in Europe to intervene when teenagers commit antisocial behaviour. For example, whereas 65 per cent of Germans, 52 per cent of Spanish and 50 per cent of Italians would be willing to intervene if they saw a group of 14-year-old boys vandalising a bus shelter, just 34 per cent of Britons would do so. These palpable fears perpetuate strongly demarcated notions of 'us' – decent, law-abiding citizens forced to invest in security to protect ourselves – and 'them' – the dangerous classes, or their offspring, who must be identified, controlled and contained.

Activity 2.1

To what extent would you say the media inform *your* knowledge and understanding of crime? Do media reports make you feel more or less secure? What other factors influence your understandings of crime?

Comment

The precise nature of the media's role in creating fear is not at all straightforward. It would be an exaggeration to say that the media are solely responsible for public insecurities about crime. Instead, it might be more accurate to say that the mainstream media reinforce what people already know about crime. Many people's feelings of vulnerability are rooted in realistic estimations of their chances of being affected by crime. Moreover, social scientists have shown through research that a previous experience of victimisation, environmental conditions, race and ethnicity, and level of confidence in the police and criminal justice system are among many of the factors that influence anxieties about crime.

In other words, attitude formation is an active process and the notion of passive audiences soaking up media influences in isolation from their lived experience is untenable. As Young (1987, p. 337) has argued, popular perceptions of crime and justice are largely 'constructed out of the material experiences of people rather than fantasies impressed upon them by the mass media'. It would also be misleading to imply that *all* media channels speak with a single voice on matters of crime and justice. *The Sun*'s approach to crime reporting is different from that of *The Independent*, and different again from that of the BBC. For some people, it may be crime reporting in *local* news media that is perceived as more alarming and anxiety provoking by virtue of its sheer proximity. Additionally, it must be remembered that growing numbers of people get their news and entertainment via the internet, where proliferating critical voices and counter-arguments offer alternative viewpoints to the dominant media interpretations of events.

Nevertheless, the role of the mass media cannot be ignored. Stan Cohen (1972) provided one of the first systematic empirical studies of the media *amplification* (i.e. the building up and exaggeration of particular social phenomena) of so-called dangerous or deviant groups and the subsequent public responses. In his case study he used the term 'moral panic' to capture the way in which skirmishes between groups of young people – 'Mods' and 'Rockers' – in seaside resorts in the 1960s were interpreted by the media and other right-minded institutions such as the police, magistrates and the business community. The groups of young people took on the role of, what he called, 'folk devils', with the implication that youth were out of control and that society was plunging into moral decline. The tendency to attribute negative social or moral trends to particular groups in the process of a moral panic is ongoing so that different groups take on the role of 'folk devil' with the arrival of new social concerns (Cohen, 1972, p. 9). Since Cohen's work, the folk devil has evolved into a more powerful icon – the 'evil monster' – perhaps most clearly exemplified by the predatory paedophile or the 'terrorist' (Jewkes, 2004). The crimes committed by these groups are, of course, serious, but identifying them in this way may make it more difficult to respond to them effectively.

Another difficulty with trying to pin down the exact nature of the media's role in creating fear is that 'fear' is notoriously difficult to define. Often conceptualised as a tangible quantity which we possess in smaller or greater amounts, fear may more accurately be thought of as consisting of a range of diffuse anxieties about one's feelings of personal safety and trust of others; in other words, *ontological* insecurity (as discussed in Chapter 1, Section 3). So, for example, women's experience of heightened anxiety in public spaces may have less to do with their actual experience of being victims of crime and more to do with their general experience of being subject to male attention and even low-level harassment. As Young (1992, p. 50) argues, 'The equivalent experience of sexual harassment for men would be if every time they walked out of doors they were met with catcalls asking if they would like a fight'. The measures that people take to avoid being victims of crime – not walking down dark alleyways, not being out alone at night, or seeking to live in safe areas – can be seen as entirely rational responses to rapid social change as a result of which the behaviour of other people seems to be much less predictable.

What is noteworthy is the extent to which the management of such risks has become privatised and devolved down to the individual: what has been referred to in the previous chapter as 'responsibilisation', or what Beck (1992, p. 100) has termed the 'individualisation of social risk'. In the realm of crime control and crime prevention, this is reflected in the extent to which homeowners are obliged to take out insurance, fit security devices and support neighbourhood watch schemes. Many of these strategies of risk avoidance can be characterised as a retreat into safe spaces, and an avoidance of those perceived to be dangerous. This chapter now turns to a consideration of the ways in which attempts are made to construct (and defend) 'safe' spaces and some of the implications that such initiatives have for policy development.

3   Public fears and social retreat

As individuals, people seek to manage risk by creating safe spaces in a variety of ways (and the next chapter critically reviews the extent to which families may be interpreted in this way). At one extreme these strategies include narrowly delimited places of retreat for personal safety, which might incorporate a range of security devices including 'panic rooms', mortise locks, barred windows, spy glass, intercom systems, arson-proof letter boxes, or silent alarms linked directly to the police. Such devices are often fitted by local authorities in the homes of women at risk from a violent partner.

At the other extreme, the drive to construct secure spaces within cities has found an expression in the interaction between a deliberate process of state-sponsored urban renewal and the apparently more market-driven processes of gentrification. The former is perhaps most apparent in the large-scale developments which have been dubbed 'mega projects' and are to be found in most major cities – in waterfront developments; in the iconic architecture of major new museums and art galleries; in the transformation of older buildings into spaces for shopping, restaurants, cafes and entertainment. This process has been nicely captured in the notion of 'pacification' or 'domestication by cappuccino' (Zukin, 1995, p. 28; Atkinson, 2003), as areas of our cities are made safe for 'coffee drinkers'. 'Gentrification' will be familiar if you watch property programmes on television, in which 'experts' advise potential property investors to look out for areas which are 'on the up', signified by the arrival of cafes, delis, organic food shops, and the like. It means the upgrading of a declining area as more middle-class people move into and renovate the existing housing stock. Gentrification can be understood as a means of encouraging neighbourhood renewal because it implies that inward investment from business will impact positively on local people, leading to a general improvement in the built environment and services.

Gentrification has, however, often also been seen as a byword for middle-class takeover, with local people being forced out by social and economic pressures and by the rising cost of housing. This has been put particularly strongly by Smith (2002, pp. 440, 442) who argues that, 'gentrification portends a displacement of working-class residents from urban centers' but also increasingly finds expression in 'more modest, neighbourhood development'. From this perspective, gentrification is seen as a process by which middle-class groups gradually colonise parts of the inner cities, mobilising their resources (and those of the banks and building societies) to do so and to benefit from the subsequent rise in property values. Like other debates in the chapter, gentrification also raises questions of social justice (see **Newman and Yeates, 2008**). And here, too, the search for security for the new residents also implies the marginalisation and policing of the old, in this case existing residents, as antisocial behaviour is first defined and then targeted.

Activity 2.2

Examine Figures 2.1 and 2.2, which represent different, but familiar, images of spaces for entertainment and eating in cities. Which picture do you think promises more security, and why?

Figure 2.1
An upmarket pub in central London

Figure 2.2

A run-down pub in central London

Comment

When we look at these images, it is hard to escape the feeling that the first represents a 'safer' and more secure environment than the second. However, it may be worth thinking a little more about what might underlie these representations: the first image may also be associated with the clearance from the local area of existing businesses and residents, through a process of gentrification. In other words, for those who were moved, this image represents *in*security. By contrast the second image may appear to be a space in which some of us might feel insecure and threatened, but for those who use it, it may represent personal security and even a means to let people like us know that this is *their* space and not 'ours'. This illustrates how senses of security may mean different things depending on where you are located, in terms of place, class, gender, ethnicity or age.

In Sections 3.1 and 3.2, two examples of 'safe spaces' of social retreat are discussed in an attempt to explore some of the consequences of the search for secure spaces. The first focuses on secure housing developments or 'gated communities', while the second considers the case of sports utility vehicles (SUVs). In Section 4, the chapter turns to consider some of the unintended effects or perverse consequences of the pursuit of security through the creation of safe spaces.

3.1 Gated communities

Some public spaces can, under certain conditions, represent places of fear and insecurity for particular individuals and groups. Urban theorist Jane Jacobs (1961) has argued that public spaces work most successfully when they provide both safety *for* strangers and safety *from* strangers. Furthermore, when brought together, strangers have the 'magical' capacity to become 'a safety asset' because they become the 'eyes on the street' and are therefore a natural form of social surveillance and mutual regulation (Jacobs, 1961, p. 46). Streets with a good mix of shops, offices, bars, clubs and cafes, in fairly constant use, work in mutually supportive, interconnected ways to enhance public safety and trust by attracting the kind of public attention, interaction, circulation, watching and listening that keeps them safe – a kind of unconscious policing.

In recent years, however, some theorists have argued that increased poverty and inequality have contributed to rising crime and violence in some urban areas, which have as a result been designated 'no-go' areas for the middle classes, the police and public administration, thus exacerbating the hold of criminality and antisocial behaviour within them. As Koonings and Kruijt (2007) note in relation to some Latin American cities:

> Urban segregation refers not only to the geographical distribution of the traditional markers of poverty (human deprivation, dilapidated housing, absent services and degraded public spaces) but also to the territorial and social division of cities in 'go' and 'no-go' areas, at least from the perspective of the middle-class citizen and local public administration. The shanty towns came to be seen as veritable enclaves that obeyed a totally different set of rules and codes of conduct.
>
> (Koonings and Kruijt, 2007, p. 12)

While this may represent one extreme, such dynamics have not been entirely absent from the UK urban landscape. In many urban areas, middle-income families and service workers (such as nurses, teachers, firefighters and police officers) have been forced out by rising house prices, leaving some inner city areas consisting of very wealthy and very poor enclaves existing side by side.

As a consequence of these new patterns of urban living and the intensified fears associated with unwanted or unpredictable juxtapositions of different people, the relatively affluent in numerous cities around the globe are opting to live in 'gated communities' – residential districts with restricted access where what normally would be public space, open to all, has been privatised; that is, made accessible only to residents. Most commonly, residents own or control communal areas, shared facilities and amenities, while simultaneously having reciprocal rights and obligations enforced by a private governing body (MacLeod, 2004). In their most extreme – though increasingly widespread – forms, gated communities are visibly guarded, fortified enclaves. While the term 'no go area' was once used to characterise only poor inner city ghettoes or shanty towns, at the beginning of the twenty-first century it can perhaps be better applied to an ever increasing number of urban neighbourhoods which are opting for *voluntary ghettoisation* (McLaughlin and Muncie, 1999). Gating may (as Manzi and Smith-Bowers, 2005, argue) be used by existing communities to control and improve their social environments in ways that make it less likely that residents will desert such areas and move out to more protected suburbs, but more often it takes the form of new development in existing neighbourhoods, and reinforces divisions between those living inside and outside their boundaries (Blandy and Lister, 2005).

Figure 2.3

Gated community in California; gated development in Bow, East London

Most gated communities have emerged in suburban areas, although increasingly they are being built in inner cities. According to Blakely and Snyder (1997), there are, broadly speaking, the following three types of gated community.

'Lifestyle Gated Communities'

These not only provide walls and gates to offer secure residential accommodation, but also exclusive access to the all-weather leisure activities and amenities within. They attract those who want to distance themselves completely from the city and who are willing to pay for separate private services and amenities. Certain 'Lifestyle Communities' have grown so popular that they have been transformed into self-contained neo-medieval cities with their own extensive shopping facilities and commercial office developments. They frequently bring together people who share a lifestyle; for example, golfing enthusiasts or retirees.

'Prestige Communities'

These are located in close proximity to cities or perhaps within gentrified or even run-down or derelict but highly valued parts of the inner city. Property developers have gone to great lengths to stress that the security-conscious architectural design will allow residents of these prime site 'urban villages' and 'city squares' to enjoy all the excitement and buzz of an urban lifestyle but with a high degree of spatial insulation from the aggravation of living in the city. 'Prestige Gated Communities' aim to appeal to the very wealthy and/or celebrities.

'Security Zone Gated Communities'

Located in inner city and inner suburb areas, 'Security Zone Gated Communities' are a third form of gated community. The origins of these particular 'walls and gates' lie with the notion of 'defensible space' developed by the American architect Oscar Newman. Newman's (1972) research in Chicago and New York suggested that the differential risks of crime and disorder that exist within and between different urban neighbourhoods were the direct result of planning and design decisions which built high density housing developments at the lowest cost and with little consideration of the social consequences. Although Newman was particularly scathing of the high-rise modernist tower block which he argued was a prime example of a residential development that had no 'defensible space', a notable trend in the UK is the gating of upgraded social housing estates as council- or housing association-owned tower blocks have been turned into gated communities, complete with high fences, an intercom system and concierge service.

In an American research study looking at the reasons behind individuals' decisions to live in a gated community, Setha Low (2003) identified several diverse motivations. A common response from inhabitants was that they were nostalgic for the past and were attempting to recreate the sense of community they remembered from their younger days. Relatedly, some occupants of gated housing referred primarily to the 'niceness' of their developments and the importance of living in a clean, graffiti-free, ordered environment where rising property prices could be relied upon. Many inhabitants identified fear of crime as their primary motivation, or specifically mentioned the desire to protect their children. Some were able to isolate fear of 'others' as their prime reason for moving to gated communities, while others talked of the importance of private governance where the community makes the rules and where conflict is resolved by the whole group (similar points were made to researchers examining the experience of gated communities in England – see Atkinson and Flint, 2004).

Activity 2.3

Read Extract 2.1 from the research study by Setha Low (2003). It concerns Felicia, a woman in her mid forties who recently moved with her husband and 7-year-old daughter to a gated community on the northern edge of San Antonio, Texas, USA. The extract is one of several narratives from interviewees that formed part of Low's research on three gated communities: one in New York, one in San Antonio, and one in Mexico City. It raises some interesting issues about the nature of 'evidence' and the value of qualitative research. In addition to interviewing residents, Low talked to 'key informants', including developers, architects, and estate agents. She also carried out observation in and around each community and had extended fieldwork visits, which entailed her living in two gated communities for a few weeks at a time. The interviews with residents are the key element of the research and form the bulk of the book from which the extract is taken. A total of fifty in-depth interviews with eighteen men and thirty-two women were conducted.

As you read Felicia's story, make notes on the following:

- Why did Felicia want to move to a gated community?

- Does the gated community really offer Felicia security, and what does she see as the drawbacks of living in these kinds of spaces?

- What has the use of these kinds of narratives as part of qualitative research allowed Low to understand? Do you think there might be any drawbacks to this kind of research method?

Extract 2.1

When they were shopping for a house, school district and aesthetics were important considerations. In fact, she had some reservations about living in a gated community, including the fact that it only has one exit if there is a fire. But they were concerned for their child's safety, and now feel that it was a good choice because it allows her to go outside and play. As Felicia puts it, 'We're in San Antonio, and I believe the whole country knows how many child-kidnappings we've had ... My husband would not ever allow her outside to play without direct adult supervision unless we were gated'. It allows them the freedom to walk around the neighborhood at night, and their daughter and her friends from nongated neighborhoods are able to ride their bicycles safely.

Felicia, however, thinks it has a flip side in that it produces a false sense of safety. The guards aren't 'Johnny-on-the-spot', and anybody who wants to could jump the gate. There's a perception of safety among residents that may not be real and could potentially leave one more vulnerable 'if there was ever an attack'. For instance, when she walks in the neighborhood, she does not look to see who is coming out of a driveway as she would on an open city street or in another suburban area. 'You don't rely on your own resources so much', she explains.

Their development is made up of people who are retired and don't want to maintain large yards, or people who want to raise families in a more protected environment. There is a lot of 'fear flight' people who have moved in the last couple of years as the crime rate, or the reporting of the crime rate, has become such a prominent part of the news. She knows people who are building because they want to get out of their exclusive subdivisions that don't have gates; she mentions one family that was shopping for a house in the gated community because they have been robbed many times.

Their neighbors are upper middle and middle class, white, Christian, and, apart from one Jewish family, quite homogeneous – businessmen and doctors, with stay-at-home wives, many without college educations. On their street, they know everyone by sight and visit with neighbors who have children; but they no longer have a party when new people move in. The houses are 'very nice', architecturally designed and custom built, and she worries that the new ones will not be as tasteful or beautiful.

Felicia feels safe inside the community, but expresses considerable anxiety about living in San Antonio:

> When I leave the area entirely and go downtown [little laugh], I feel quite threatened just being out in normal urban areas, unrestricted urban areas ... Please let me explain. The north central part of this city [San Antonio], by and large, is middle-class to upper-middle class. Period. There are very few pockets of poverty. Very few. And therefore if you go to any store, you will look around and most of the clientele will be middle class as you are yourself. So you're somewhat insulated. But if you go downtown, which is more mixed, where everybody goes, I feel much more threatened.

Her daughter was four years old when they first moved, and I wonder about the psychological impact of moving from a rambling, unfenced Californian suburb to a gated community. Felicia says her daughter feels threatened when she sees poor people because she hasn't had enough exposure:

> We were driving next to a truck with some day labourers and equipment in the back, and we were stopped behind them at a light. She wanted to move because she was afraid those people were going

to come and get her. They looked scary to her. I explained that they were workmen, they're the 'backbone of our country', they're coming from work, you know, but ...

So living in a secured enclave may heighten a child's fear of others. It's unclear, though, whether Felicia's observation reflects many children's experience of growing up in a gated community, or simply her daughter's idiosyncrasy and modelling of her mother's anxiety.

Felicia and her husband wanted to buy the nicest house in the best school district, while providing a safe environment for their daughter, one where they can be cloistered from class differences. They consider the neighborhood 'a real community' where you know your neighbors, although it is not as friendly as where they used to live. For them, the gated community provides a haven in a socially and culturally diverse world, offering a protected setting for their upper-middle-class lifestyle.

Low, 2003, pp. 8–9

Comment

Felicia's reasons for moving to a gated community ranged from fears of crime and violence, particularly fears for her child, and that the community had the 'right' kind of schools, religious values and respectable and traditional families; families that exemplify a narrow social stratum – the professional middle classes. It also offers the chance of a 'real community' where people know each other because of their social similarity and their comparative freedom to move about, at least within the protected enclave of the gated community (for wider discussion of the role of community in the pursuit of crime control and social welfare, see **Mooney and Neal, 2009**). She does note some clear drawbacks from the point of view of safety and security. Being less aware of potential dangers, she is not on her guard, and, given that the gated development offers only a fantasy of security, this could be dangerous. Her daughter has also become more fearful, as she has been shielded from some of life's complications, such as an experience of poverty. Lastly, Felicia expresses concern that the community might not be heading in a positive direction, because of the building of more unattractive buildings, or because people are less friendly than they used to be.

The model of homogeneous (sub)urban living put forward in this narrative is the antithesis to the ideal envisaged by Jacobs (1961, pp. 250–1) who believed that diversity and a degree of benign disorder associated with the presence of strangers are crucial for the vitality and safety of public places: 'Areas flourishing in diversity sprout strange and unpredictable uses and peculiar scenes. But this is not a drawback of diversity. This is the point or part of it.' In an environment where diversity is avoided, far less desired, the other side of the coin is inevitably systematic structural exclusion (Young, 2007). Fear has the capacity to unite people: a phenomenon illustrated by Felicia in San Antonio and her fellow occupants of gated communities who yearn for a 'privatopia' in which 'property rights and property values are the focus of community life; and where homogeneity, exclusiveness, and exclusion are the foundation of social organization' (McKenzie, 1996, p. 177).

It is also evident from Felicia's account, however, that living in a secure gated community can, paradoxically, generate feelings of insecurity, both within the secure perimeter (because of the highly visible security measures which serve as symbolic reminders of perceived threats) and on the occasions when one has to travel beyond the community's gates. Finally, the extract underlines the point made in Section 2 that the media undoubtedly play a part in fuelling people's anxieties – some residents of the gated community moved there because of fears generated by news reports – but that personal experience is at least as important – one family wished to move there because they had been 'robbed many times'.

Extract 2.1 provides qualitative evidence to illustrate the complexities of contemporary debates about welfare and crime control policies. The research study from which the reading is taken demonstrates that these kinds of research methods – in this case, one-to-one interviewing in the respondent's home – encourage the interviewee to speak freely in a safe space, and allow the researcher to explore the motivations behind, and consequences of, the respondent's choices and behaviour. As a research site, the gated community lends itself well to qualitative research precisely because it is 'contained' and separated from the wider environs. It is therefore relatively easy to research the different motivations of the affluent middle classes who live in such developments. By contrast, it is much more difficult to research qualitatively the effects and impacts of displacement on the working-class communities cleared away from areas where gentrification has occurred and gated communities have developed, simply because it is so difficult to track a dispersed group of people. A further potential drawback of qualitative studies is that the findings are based on subjective responses from a small number of interviewees rather than supposedly more objective data such as official statistics or wider surveys (but see Chapter 4 for discussion of some of the challenges associated with the use of official and survey data), which is one reason why qualitative evidence is frequently not mobilised in policymaking. The concluding chapter of this book returns to this dilemma.

3.2 Sports utility vehicles

Often referred to as the vehicular form of a gated community because of its sturdy looks and seemingly impregnable security features, the 'sports utility vehicle' or 'SUV' is a description imported from the USA and, although 'four-by-four' or 'off-road vehicle' are terms more commonly used in the UK, the ascription 'SUV' will be used throughout the discussion that follows because it highlights the fact that the vehicles in question have a range of capabilities that cross between work (utility) and leisure (sport/pleasure) (Wells, 2006). Historically, the market for such vehicles was constrained by the engineering choices required to meet the requirements of off-road performance, which resulted in relatively slow, noisy, crude and cumbersome vehicles when applied to everyday on-road use. The vehicles also tended to be characterised by an absence of 'comfort' features considered desirable in a car required for everyday use. However, more recently, manufacturers have sought to combine off-road capabilities with the characteristics expected of mainstream cars, thereby broadening market appeal. The SUV is now one of the most popular types of vehicle in the UK and elsewhere, a trend that has continued despite growing concerns about the impact of such 'gas guzzlers' on the environment. Although rising fuel costs may now be reducing their attractiveness for some, by 2005, the number of SUVs sold in the UK had reached 187,000, compared with 80,000 a decade before. They accounted for almost 8 per cent, or one in 15, of all cars sold, and that figure rose to 1 in 7 in major cities such as London (Wells, 2006).

Figure 2.4

A family on the school run in their four-by-four

Activity 2.4

■ First, if you are able, search the internet sites of companies such as Land Rover, Nissan, Toyota and the manufacturers of the Hummer, and look at how they advertise their SUVs. What kinds of values are they attempting to convey through these ads? How do these experiences compare with your own experience of SUVs (as an owner, passenger, fellow road user, cyclist or pedestrian)?

■ Now, read the following extract from Josh Lauer's (2005) research on the rise of SUVs in the USA, which systematically analyses promotional material, newspaper and magazine articles. As you read, make notes on the values embodied by the sports utility vehicle that are identified in the article. How do they resemble or differ from the attributes you may have noted in relation to the advertisements?

Extract 2.2

The notion that SUVs are exceptionally safe vehicles is largely due to their four-wheel-drive capability, which provides good handling in bad weather, and their tall profile, which grants drivers a panoramic view of the road and emerging traffic patterns. However, mainstream coverage of SUVs and SUV advertisements themselves suggest that the safety justification is more broadly an appeal to a militaristic sense of security, self defense, and invincibility. ... [As an article in the *New York Times* notes] the interiors of new SUVs may exude luxury and comfort – feminine warmth and procreation – but the exteriors remain masculine, intimidating, and warlike ...

...

The association with military conquest is a common feature of advertising in both trade and popular journalism involving SUVs. An ad for Toyota Land Cruiser [in the *National Geographic*], for example, touts the vehicle's 'commanding presence' ... Another for Chevy Blazer [in *Ward's Automotive Yearbook*] reads: 'Tough Chevy trucks are taking charge' ... SUVs suggest that their owners are not only unafraid, but actively engaged in defending themselves. They are aggressively defensive. According to one review [in the *Washington Post*]: 'the 1989 Range Rover is neither car nor truck. It's a luxury tank, a metro war wagon' ... A reviewer of the Jeep Cherokee Sport [in the same newspaper] tellingly revealed: 'I know why many Americans own guns. It's the same reason they own four-wheel-drive, sport-utility vehicles. It's G.A.P.S. – the Great American Potency Syndrome, the need to have more than is needed, just in case' ...

...

While advertisements for SUVs typically feature their capability in outback settings, these images of rocky badlands and impenetrable forests often serve as a metaphor for society and, in particular, the city. They suggest that civilization itself is an inhospitable environment, an urban jungle. This connection is glibly invoked in many SUV advertisements. The headline of one ad [in the *New Yorker*], featuring the image of a Toyota 4Runner parked in front of a city brownstone, states: 'It's the only 4-wheel drive to have in this neck of the woods'. The ad also notes that the 4Runner is 'the ideal way to make tracks in the urban jungle' ... A slightly paranoid Chevy S-10 Blazer ad [in the *National Geographic*] attempts to reassure its prospective drivers:

> But for all its social acceptance, we've never forgotten Blazer's reason for being: a rugged, maneuverable 4WD truck intended to get you away from the ordinary. And carry you high, dry and serenely through situations that are the stuff of both dreams and nightmares ... [It] will make your heart beat faster. And not out of fright. But out of fun ...

Yet another ad [also in the *National Geographic*], one for GMC Jimmy, portrays a desolate, pothole-riddled road with a cityscape beyond. The copy reads: 'So you can go boldly ... where a mere sports car would fear to travel' ...

In addition to their imposing size and protective shells, SUVs also offer a useful aspect of social camouflage, enabling the well-to-do to 'pass' as regular working folk in urban settings. For example, an MTV executive [quoted in *Forbes* magazine] who travels to 'fringe neighborhoods' in search of new talent admits that 'he feels less conspicuous in a Jeep than in a Mercedes' ... In Hollywood, the early 1990s trend toward 'downscale' vehicles is reflected in the popularity of SUVs. Some entertainment executives [reported in the *New York Times*] cite the personal hazard of driving luxury cars, especially flashy sports cars, in 'crime-vulnerable Los Angeles' as an explanation for Hollywood's attraction to Range Rovers with headlight 'rhino-guards' ...

Despite such add-on exterior excesses, the SUV is capable of suggesting a working-class solidarity and populism that enables their mostly white-collar professional drivers to appropriate a marker of 'authentic' manual labor and recreation. This aspect of authenticity, along with the SUV's large, rugged exteriors, provides a passive deterrence factor. Commenting on the interior opulence beneath their rugged exteriors, one reviewer [in the *Washington Post*] notes: 'Some sport utility vehicles offer voice-activated cellular telephones and compact disc players, plus an option that enables owners to hide them. It's not clear whether that feature is attractive to discourage theft or to avoid the appearance of snobbishness' ...

...

The idea of privileged space is also evoked in juxtapositions of country and urban living, a common motif in SUV advertising. The image of town and country gentility conjures a fantasy of landed aristocrats with gated city homes and spacious country retreats, with the SUV at home in both. At the same time, the SUV's populist aura is appropriated in the guise of the self-reliant woodsman, which diffuses and rationalizes any overt indication of class superiority by suggesting that one's self-selected solitude is a confrontation with nature rather than society. This privileged aesthetic is also reflected in the simultaneous popularity of rustic outdoor sport and hunting clothes during the 1980s, exemplified by companies such as L.L. Bean, Ralph Lauren, J. Crew, and Banana Republic. A *Newsweek* ... article identifying this fashion trend includes a segment on Land Rover: 'Long the preferred country car of the European aristocracy, the Range Rover now reigns as essential equipment for every would-be American squire' ...

...

While projecting a facade of confident social mastery, SUVs were more tellingly presented as a means to retreat from the maddening crowd. This is part and parcel of the 'lifestyle' dimension so often attributed to consumer interest in SUVs. Like its association with soldiers, tough outdoorsmen, and country squires, driving an SUV suggests one's freedom to be outside, to put social distance between oneself and others at will. The SUV's ability to traverse the world's most inhospitable terrain is another way of suggesting that one can – and must – go to extremes to escape one's fellows. One ad [in the *National Geographic*] features a Jeep Grand Cherokee perched on a desolate rocky ridge with the following copy: 'How on Earth do you lose 5.6 billion people?' ... SUV owners are not necessarily rushing to nature, but fleeing 'a world of risky strangers' (Furedi, 1997).

Lauer, 2005, pp. 158–62

Comment

Lauer observes that promotional images like the ones you may have been able to access on the internet characteristically feature the SUV's capability both in wide-open spaces and in the urban jungle. These images might indicate to you values such as ruggedness, freedom, comfort, luxury, or any number of other 'positive' attributes, and, as

Lauer (2005, p. 150) observes, the SUV is always argued to be a superior driving experience because of its 'practicality'. As Lauer's analysis of advertising for SUVs in Extract 2.2 has shown, however, the SUV has other, perhaps more suspect, associations – military conquest, a way of protecting occupants from the urban 'jungle', a camouflage for the wealthy as they drive through poorer areas, reflecting ideas of status and of putting distance betweens themselves and the world. The use of SUVs may, in other words, be associated with a vision of social space that is

> linked by patterns of movement which are detached from their social contexts, promoting a cognitive map of the city inhabited by like-minded individuals that generate socially homogeneous contact absent of potential threats and encounters. The dependence on, and use of cars can be seen as an extension of gating ... – the orchestrated management of perceived risk spaces and social contact while moving around the public realm in shielded corridors.
>
> (Atkinson and Flint, 2004, p. 889)

For Lauer, the popularity of SUVs reflects key developments in contemporary American culture:

- A fear of crime and violence disproportionate – given the falling crime rate in American cities – to the likelihood of being a victim of crime. It is fear of crime in particular that appears to be behind the growing prevalence of the SUV; market research conducted by the automobile industry underlines that this is the critical factor distinguishing purchasers of SUVs from demographically identical purchasers of minivans (Simon, 2002).

- The way that risk has become individualised (responsibilised) into a personal struggle for survival in the 'inhospitable terrain' of the city.

- Because the management of risk has become privatised and individualised, safety – whether real or symbolic – has become synonymous with money and status. Put simply, money protects. As Lauer argues, 'the SUV, like gentrification and gated communities, implicitly rationalized the economic segregation of public space and the unequal allocation of natural resources – all in the name of personal risk management' (2005, pp. 165–6).

4   Security, insecurity and the search for safe spaces

So far, this chapter has discussed public fears and insecurities and the privatisation and individualisation of responsibility for protecting ourselves from risk. It should be noted, however, that 'fear' need not always be a bad thing. On a broader level, the authors of the British Crime Survey have argued that a 'certain level of concern or wariness' is beneficial in encouraging people to take measures to reduce their risk of victimisation (Kershaw et al., 2000, p. 50). The identification of some risks that have previously been overlooked may also redress the balance, with one set of fears being set against another set. So, for example, in the case of SUVs, public and political opposition to 'gas guzzling' vehicles – frequently articulated in the pages of the popular press – highlights the damage being done to the environment: an issue that has achieved global acknowledgement only in relatively recent years.

However, the social changes outlined in this chapter may also have some 'perverse consequences'. Put simply, gated communities and SUVs provide their occupants with daily palpable reminders of the very risks they seek to evade. As a result, there is a danger that the latest attempts to de-intensify urban space will result in the emergence of 'fortress cities' riddled with sharply demarcated, privatised, walled and gated enclaves. In such a climate, visible surveillance technologies may further increase public anxieties and contribute to the image of public spaces as dangerous places. Paradoxically, the solution most frequently put forward to counter the public insecurity that is, in part, generated by the prevalence of surveillance systems is to introduce yet more surveillance systems. Hence a greater level of exclusion is created and a 'fortress mentality' of segregation is reinforced. In some countries with very high rates of violent crime (South Africa and Brazil, for example), the pursuit of 'total security' has become a way of life – but only for those who can afford it: 'Most people living in enclosed areas no longer make use of the streets, and public spaces are no longer used and shared by all urban residents. These spaces are now abandoned to the poor, the homeless and street children, who are left vulnerable to violence and abuse by various control groups, including criminals and the security forces' (Landman and Schönteich, 2002, p. 80).

Activity 2.5

This chapter has used examples from research conducted in the context of the USA and Latin America. Do you see any equivalents in the UK context? What might be some of the differences between the USA, Latin America and the UK? When thinking about these questions, read Extract 2.3 by freelance journalist Philip Hensher who is comparing Battersea, London, with Sao Paulo, Brazil.

Extract 2.3

On the Battersea street where I live, a former school has been transformed into a gated community. You can see cars drive in and out, but hardly ever do you see anyone walking out to the local shops. I know quite a few people who live on my road but literally nobody within the development. They are quite simply sealed off from the community. The area is not dangerous in the slightest, and it is difficult to understand quite why the local authority agreed to a development which could lead to a degree of social isolation when no significant crime rate could easily justify it.

I don't think there's any doubt that the rich and the poor are drawing from the same well of social cohesion. By demanding a completely unreasonable degree of security and protection within cities which, by any standard, are still remarkably safe to live in, the rich are withdrawing from the local economic and social life, and in the long run making the lives of others more difficult.

... [I]f we don't know our neighbours, don't invest in local businesses, and travel about in our own cars, then the end result will look like Sao Paulo. We shouldn't be under any illusion: that wall separating the tennis-playing middle classes from the crime-ridden and vulnerable urban masses, living in shacks of their own construction, is not a measured response to a difficult situation, but in the last analysis, a substantial contribution to the situation itself.

(Hensher, 2006)

Comment

This is a powerful piece of journalism. Hensher sets out to warn us of the possible consequences for collective security if the fearful middle classes attempt to seal themselves off from the mass of society and withdraw from day-to-day (economic and social) interaction with others in the neighbourhood in which they live. He uses the iconic image of Sao Paulo to reinforce his arguments – the threat of looking like Sao Paulo is presented as a real (and immediate) one. However, the evidence on which Hensher draws is limited: we learn little about life in Sao Paulo and the process by which the creation of one gated community in Battersea will lead to a more generalised breakdown of urban life is uncertain. Nevertheless, the article succeeds in highlighting the point that historically mixed and diverse urban areas are not immune from attempts to construct barriers, reinforcing the argument that creating divisions may be part of the problem rather than the solution.

The popularity of SUVs may also generate increased insecurity. The World Health Organization estimated that 1.2 million people are killed in road crashes each year and as many as 50 million are injured (WHO, 2004). Projections indicate that these figures will increase by about 65 per cent over the next twenty years, which would then make car crashes the third biggest cause of death globally. According to a study by the US Insurance Institute for Highway Safety (IIHS), there are many more deaths from crashes involving SUVs than any other vehicles. For all crashes between cars and SUVs, people in cars are about four times more likely to die than people inside SUVs. The IIHS report also states that when SUVs strike cars in the side, the risk of death for car occupants relative to the risk of the SUV occupants dying is 27 to 1 (IIHS, 1998). Because of the greater height of an SUV, the point of impact tends to be higher than the bumpers of ordinary cars, particularly in collisions with children where head and chest injuries are more common than leg and lower body injuries. SUVs have a stiffer chassis than other cars, which means there is no 'crumple zone' with which to absorb impact. They are twice as likely to cause severe traumatic brain and abdominal injuries and 50 per cent more likely to kill the passenger of another vehicle. And while it is important to recognise that the UK has a good road safety record overall compared with many other countries, Wells (2006) notes that if drivers of these large four-wheel-drive vehicles feel 'safer' as is often reported, it is not unreasonable to expect other drivers to feel less safe in normal passenger cars. As a result, he suggests, there is a danger that all purchasers of new cars will seek to acquire larger vehicles than would otherwise be the case, in order to feel 'competitive' on the road.

It is perhaps ironic, then, that many consumers buy SUVs to accommodate their new and growing families. While many parents have invested in SUVs primarily to drive themselves and their children around in comfort and safety, many commentators including the World Health Organization are concerned that these vehicles make a considerable contribution to global warming, are responsible for tens of thousands of premature deaths in Western Europe alone each year, including children, and play a significant role in emerging health crises including growing numbers of cases of childhood asthma and other respiratory illnesses.

Hidden behind the entrenched ideology of American car culture, the automobile's criminality is, according to Ferrell (2002, p. 195), manifest in 'the daily victimization of passengers, pedestrians, and bicyclists by the thousands'. As Lauer argues:

> While the media and the public obsess over topical issues such as car jacking, road rage, defective Firestone tyres, sleepy drivers, drug-addled car thieves, cell phone distracted drivers, and OPEC's

manipulation of oil prices, cars in the US – and SUVs in particular –
continue to exact a daily body count and environmental toll that,
in relative terms, elicits little controversy.

(Lauer, 2005, p. 165)

The disputed status of their security credentials is exemplified by the fact
that *What Car?* magazine chose a model of the Land Rover Discovery as
its Car of the Year 2005, describing it both as a 'family-friendly' vehicle
and as a 'hard-as-nails 4 × 4' (*What Car?*, 2005). More unequivocally, the
New Economic Foundation's policy director, Andrew Simms, has said of
SUVs, 'They're really Satan's little run-around' (quoted in Black, 2004).

Forms of privatised security such as gated communities and the SUV
may also have other detrimental qualities. It was noted in Activity 2.3
that one of the reasons Felicia opted to live in a gated community was to
protect her child; paradoxically, however, she observed that her child
was becoming perhaps less able to deal with other types of people. The
popularity of the SUV is often cited by users to be about protecting their
children; hence their controversial use has been noted on the
'school run'. However, in trying to protect children from risk some
commentators have argued that the SUV also protects children from
development, which arises from a freedom to roam. Thus Furedi
(1997, p. 115) argues that in recent years society has seen a 'major
reorganization of the childhood experience ... [whereby] roaming about
with friends or walking to and from school are becoming increasingly
rare experiences'.

5   Review

This chapter has explored the relationship between emergent cultures of
fear and the privatisation of some risks, which exemplifies the idea of
responsibilisation explored in Chapter 1. Following this chapter's
discussion in Section 2 about media-fuelled moral panics concerning
high profile yet atypical crimes, it is interesting to note that both
Setha Low and Josh Lauer refer to the profusion of violent media images
as a key source of generalised anxiety. As noted previously, the long-term
effects of exposure to mediated images of crime are virtually impossible
to gauge and we should be cautious when making statements about
the media 'causing' fear and insecurity. However, it is also worth
bearing in mind that fear of crime is a much more widely experienced
phenomenon than victimisation – that is, an actual experience of crime.
Although victims of crime will probably become more anxious about the
likelihood of future victimisation as a result of their experiences, many
more individuals will experience fear as a result of indirect contact with
crime. These vicarious experiences of crime will encompass personal
observations, private conversations with victims, second-, third- and

fourth-hand accounts passed down through varied and diverse flows of communication, *and* exposure to, and interaction with, the media. Thus influenced by a variety of pressures and incentives to take responsibility for their own protection, victims and potential victims are seduced into assessing their risk, modifying their behaviour, investing in expensive technology and creating 'safe spaces' of social retreat.

This chapter has explored some of the consequences of these processes. Paradoxically, the gentrification of inner city areas is founded on the perception that certain groups of people – such as young professionals or families – want to live in communities characterised by a degree of diversity (however superficial or idealised that aspiration might be in reality), yet the process itself encourages a tendency towards homogeneity and segregation because of the fear of the crime and violence associated with other, perhaps marginalised, social groups. Some urban spaces are transformed, as inner city housing, factories, warehouses, docklands and even prisons are gentrified or turned into prime real estate. At the same time, in the relatively deprived spaces in between, overcrowding, homelessness and crime continue to rise.

Meanwhile, for those who opt to live in newly developed gated communities, any notion of living in a diverse community is regarded not only as unattainable but possibly also as undesirable. Critics of gated communities point out that it is a mistake to view them as simply shifting the balance of power, in the way that broader forms of gentrification might be said to do. With other forms of gentrification, while the city's existing working-class population will feel the squeeze when it comes to housing, in areas such as education they still have a stake and therefore there is a balance of power to be contested. With gated communities, however, it is more likely a case of outright appropriation as space is taken away by developers for the benefit of a community that has no intention of making any significant contact with the local population.

Qualitative research evidence has enabled us to explore the extent to which individuals who live in gated, secure communities and drive SUVs are seeking simultaneous feelings of security, control and escape. Such individuals lead a kind of urban lifestyle, but one that avoids the harsh reality of urban life and, instead, offers a protective cocoon. Yet, while those who drive SUVs or live behind electronic gates might not unreasonably claim that doing so makes them feel more secure, it is equally plausible that, for many people, security measures inculcate a sense of fear, not only of victimisation but also of being watched, ordered, controlled, criminalised. Lucia Zedner illustrates some of the ways in which concerns about security paradoxically serve to heighten feelings of vulnerability:

The home owner who sets her alarm each time she leaves the house is constantly reminded of the possibility of burglary during her absence. Likewise the ubiquitous signs warning that property is mark-protected, that CCTV cameras are in operation, or guards patrolling are akin to anxiety makers advertising the risks of crime at every turn ... Likewise sports utility vehicles (SUVs) are made the subject of aggressive marketing campaigns that emphasise their bullish capacity to protect their passengers from unknown external threats ... Paradoxically, the subjective security created by the armoured environment of the SUV only exacerbates the sense of personal vulnerability encountered on leaving the vehicle. Hence the proliferation in the United States of drive-in fast food joints that do not require one to risk even the few meters between car and restaurant ... Personal segregation, whether in cars, suburban residential communities, doorman-protected apartment buildings, or exclusive leisure facilities is predicated upon risks 'out there' ... The more provision for security that is made, the more people regard it as normal or necessary, and the greater their anxiety when it is not available. And for those who cannot afford to buy into these 'bubbles of security' in the first place, the sense of standing outside protection, of inhabiting dangerous places only increases.

(Zedner, 2003, pp. 165–6)

There may, then, be certain perverse consequences of the social changes and segregation policies outlined in this chapter. The remaining chapters in this book go on to explore the nature of 'security' as a slippery but evocative concept and one that promises to deliver much, but may instead serve also to reinforce *in*security.

Further reading

If you are interested in further exploring the relationship between media and crime, then my book on *Media and Crime* (2004, Sage) provides a comprehensive introduction and review. Some of the tensions between security and insecurity in the attempt to create safe spaces are further explored in an article by Lucia Zedner (2003) 'Too much security?', *International Journal of the Sociology of Law* (vol. 31, no. 3, pp. 155–84). For a critical review of the impact of the culture of fear on the way in which people live their lives today, you may want to read Frank Furedi's *Culture of Fear: Risk-Taking and the Morality of Low Expectation* (1997, Cassell).

References

Atkinson, R. (2003) 'Domestication by cappuccino or a revenge on urban space? Control and empowerment in the management of public spaces', *Urban Studies*, vol. 40, no. 9, pp. 1829–43.

Atkinson, R. and Flint, J. (2004) 'Fortress UK? Gated communities, the spatial revolt of the elites and time–space trajectories of segregation', *Housing Studies*, vol. 19, no. 6, pp. 875–92.

Beck, U. (1992) *Risk Society*, London, Sage.

Black, A. (2004) '4 × 4s "should carry health warning"', BBC News, 26 November [online], http://news.bbc.co.uk/1/hi/sci/tech/4043959.stm (Accessed 2 January 2008).

Blakely, E.J. and Snyder, M.G. (1997) *Fortress America: Gated Communities in the United States*, Washington, DC, Brookings Institution Press.

Blandy, S. and Lister, D. (2005) 'Gated communities: (ne)gating community development?', *Housing Studies*, vol. 20, no. 2, pp. 287–301.

Cohen, S. (1972) *Folk Devils and Moral Panics: The Creation of Mods and Rockers*, London, MacGibbon & Kee.

Ferrell, J. (2002) *Tearing Down the Streets*, London, Palgrave Macmillan.

Furedi, F. (1997) *Culture of Fear: Risk-Taking and the Morality of Low Expectation*, London, Cassell.

Girling, E., Loader, I. and Sparks, R. (2000) *Crime and Social Change in Middle England: Questions of Order in an English Town*, London, Routledge.

Hensher, P. (2006) 'Gated communities are promoting irrational fears', *The Independent*, 26 September [online], http://comment.independent.co.uk/commentators/philip_hensher/article1757240.ece (Accessed 2 January 2008).

Insurance Institute for Highway Safety (IIHS) (1998) *New Study of Relationships Between Vehicle Weight and Occupant Death Rates Helps Put in Perspective Issue of Crash Compatibility*, news release, 10 February [online], http://www.iihs.org/news/1998/iihs_news_021098.pdf (Accessed 2 January 2008).

Jacobs, J. (1961) *The Death and Life of Great American Cities*, Harmondsworth, Penguin.

Jewkes, Y. (2004) *Media and Crime*, London, Sage.

Kershaw, C., Budd, T., Kinshott, G., Mattinson, J., Mayhew, P. and Myhill, A. (2000) *The 2000 British Crime Survey*, Home Office Statistical Bulletin 18/00, London, Home Office; also available online at http://www.homeoffice.gov.uk/rds/pdfs/hosb1800.pdf (Accessed 2 Janaury 2008).

Koonings, K. and Kruijt, D. (2007) 'Fractured cities, second-class citizenship and urban violence' in Koonings, K. and Kruijt, D. (eds) *Fractured Cities: Social Exclusion, Urban Violence and Contested Spaces in Latin America*, London, Zed Books.

Landman, K. and Schönteich, M. (2002) 'Urban fortresses: gated communities as a reaction to crime', *African Security Review*, vol. 11, no. 4, pp. 71–85.

Lauer, J. (2005) 'Driven to extremes: fear of crime and the rise of the sport utility vehicle in the United States', *Crime, Media, Culture*, vol. 1, no. 2, pp. 149–68.

Low, S. (2003) *Behind the Gates: Life, Security and the Pursuit of Happiness in Fortress America*, New York, NY, Routledge.

MacLeod, G. (2004) *Privatizing the City? The Tentative Push Towards Edge Urban Developments and Gated Communities in the United Kingdom*, Final Report for the Office of the Deputy Prime Minister, International Centre for Regional Regeneration and Development Studies, Stockton, University of Durham.

McKenzie, E. (1996) *Privatopia: Homeowner Associations and the Rise of Residential Private Government*, New Haven, CT, Yale University Press.

McLaughlin, E. and Muncie, J. (1999) 'Walled cities: surveillance, regulation and segregation' in Pile, S., Brook, C. and Mooney, G. (eds) *Unruly Cities? Order/Disorder*, London, Routledge.

Manzi, T. and Smith-Bowers, B. (2005) 'Gated communities as club goods: segregation or social cohesion? *Housing Studies*, vol. 20, no. 2, pp. 345–59.

Margo, J. and Dixon, M. (2006) 'Crisis of youth? Childhood, youth and civic order', *Public Policy Research*, vol. 13, issue 1, pp. 48–53.

Mooney, G. (2008) '"Problem" populations, "problem" places' in Newman, J. and Yeates, N. (eds) *Social Justice: Welfare, Crime and Society*, Maidenhead, Open University Press/Milton Keynes, The Open University.

Mooney, G. and Neal, S. (eds) (2009) *Community: Welfare, Crime and Society*, Maidenhead, Open University Press/Milton Keynes, The Open University.

Newman, J. and Yeates, N. (eds) (2008) *Social Justice: Welfare, Crime and Society*, Maidenhead, Open University Press/Milton Keynes, The Open University.

Newman, O. (1972) *Defensible Space: People and Design in the Violent City*, London, Architectural Press.

Simon, J. (2002) 'Guns, crime and governance', *Houston Law Review*, vol. 39, no. 1, pp. 133–48.

Smith, N. (2002) 'New globalism, new urbanism: gentrification as global urban strategy', *Antipode*, vol. 34, no. 3, pp. 427–50.

Wells, P. (2006) *Off-Road Car, On-Road Menace*, London, Greenpeace.

What Car? (2005) 'Car of the year 2005' [online], 21 January, http://www.whatcar.co.uk/news-special-report.aspx?NA=213136&EL=3111043 (Accessed 27 February 2008).

World Health Organization (WHO) (2004) 'Road safety: a public health issue' [online], http://www.who.int/features/2004/road_safety/en/ (Accessed 27 February 2008).

Young, J. (1987) 'The tasks facing a realist criminology', *Contemporary Crises*, vol. 11, pp. 337–56.

Young, J. (1992) 'Ten points of realism' in Young, J. and Matthews, R. (eds) *Rethinking Criminology: The Realist Debate*, London, Sage.

Young, J. (2007) *The Vertigo of Late Modernity*, London, Sage.

Zedner, L. (2003) 'Too much security?', *International Journal of the Sociology of Law*, vol. 31, no. 3, pp. 155–84.

Zukin, S. (1995) *The Cultures of Cities*, Oxford, Blackwell.

Chapter 3
Security, insecurity and family lives

Jane Ribbens McCarthy

Contents

1   Introduction

The previous chapter looked at the ways in which some people seek to develop spaces in which they can feel more secure and less vulnerable to risks that they perceive to be a threat in contemporary Western societies. The old adage that 'an Englishman's home is his castle' perhaps reflects a longer-standing view that homes, and families within them, constitute one such key site of security. However, while the reference to homes and castles points towards the significance of physical space, family and home are not, of course, synonymous. Families may spill across and beyond 'the home' (and some families may be home-less). In other words, families are not so easily identifiable as clearly bounded units. Furthermore, the gendered and nationalistic language of this old saying alerts us to the fact that other (power) dynamics – such as gender, ethnicity and generation – may complicate the picture, while references to 'castles' point to issues of class and inequality in achieving this ideal. Indeed, much feminist writing in recent decades has been concerned to reveal just what an idealised picture is often (implicitly) assumed in representations and social policies concerning family lives, even if these may also be ideals which people themselves hold dear, and seek to perpetuate.

Issues of power dynamics within and between families point to a key paradox, then, which this chapter will explore, concerning the ways in which families can be understood to constitute both a site of security and also of insecurity for *individual members*. Most obviously, individuals may look to families for physical security, including food, warmth, sexual contact, and basic care when dependent on others, as well as social and emotional contact and bonding at the deepest levels. Furthermore, in their family interactions over time, individuals may develop a shared sense of what is 'normal daily life', in the process creating microcosms of social order in specific localised contexts – even if such order may be contingent, fragile and constantly open to negotiation. But if families hold the possibility of providing individuals with (ontological) security in all these various ways, they also hold the possibility of failing to provide such security, and indeed, this failure can extend to significant risk and insecurity, including abuse and harm at the most fundamental levels.

But families are not just a 'private' or 'personal' matter – they are also often seen as a fundamental *building block of social life*, the means by which children learn to become social beings and responsible citizens and workers, and through which adults are expected to find a stable part to play in social life, not least because of their association with notions of community (see **Mooney and Neal, 2009**). Families are thus often understood as key sites where public policy matters on the one hand, and private, personal, matters on the other, coincide, so that they *either*

Figure 3.1

Families may be living in a great variety of circumstances: a miner and his family at a welfare centre during the UK miners' strike, 1984; an HIV-positive father, who is being treated with antiretroviral medication, poses with his family outside their home in South Africa; an orphaned family, headed by a 15-year-old boy, collecting water in a rural community in Swaziland; a Japanese family taking a young girl to a Shinto shrine in Kyoto for a festival to celebrate children aged 3 to 7

confront one another in ways that create difficulties for law and order, *or* work together to produce social order for society, and personal satisfaction and security for individuals. So family life becomes a mechanism by which governments seek to deliver security, even as families may also at times be seen as a source of disorder when they fail to produce these goods for society more generally. As such, families can be seen to have a crucial part to play in relation to issues of crime and social order. This is the second paradox, then, that will constitute a key thread for this chapter, concerning the part that families may play for *society at large* in delivering *both* security and insecurity.

Features of social structure, however, such as class and inequality, 'race' and ethnicity, point us towards a further key tension, about the differences *between* families, in terms of the wider resources available to family members. These differences may have crucial implications for how (far) particular families are experienced as a basis for (in)security. Such resources will most obviously include financial and material income, but they may also include more social resources – such as kinship or friendship networks, locality and neighbourhood – which may provide knowledge, information and support of varying kinds, as well as cultural resources, which may privilege certain assumptions or expectations of family life as 'normal' and thus 'better'. In many situations, however, families lack security at the most fundamental level of physical safety, as, for example, when struggling to survive in areas of conflict such as some parts of Africa or the Middle East, or in conditions of extreme poverty (as discussed in Chapter 5). As well as being a *source* of security, then, families may also be *in need* of security, if the welfare of family members is to be assured, and this is the third key paradox running through this chapter.

These pervasive paradoxes create some core tensions for how we understand family lives, including questions about how families can be researched – to capture both the particularities and commonalities of people's diverse personal experiences – and questions about how we theorise and evaluate families in more general terms. Such tensions mean that families are understood in very variable ways: as idealised or demonised; as the basis of social order or the reproduction of social inequalities; as creators of useful future citizens or troublesome future criminals.

The aims of this chapter are to:

- consider the notion of 'family' as a problematic but key concept in social policies and a meeting point between personal lives and social policies

- identify and explore the tensions within families as sites of security and insecurity, particularly as they affect parents and children

- consider how issues of age, gender, generation, class and ethnicity are key dimensions for understanding 'families'

- understand how cultural and material issues may significantly shape experiences of (in)security in families

- review some of the complexities of researching these ambiguous and sensitive issues, particularly through the textual analysis of policy documents.

Activity 3.1

Look back to Chapter 1, to consider the opening list (in Activity 1.1) of the different ways in which security seems to be commonly understood. Look through this list and consider how far, and in what ways, families may be implicated in each form of security.

Comment

It seems to me that families are likely to be significantly involved, in various ways, in all the forms of security listed. Even national and international security is likely to be stronger where family resources can meet the survival and welfare needs of family members. And families may well play a crucial part in enhancing environmental security; for example, through health care, or through efforts to minimise use of scarce environmental resources. Different societies and political systems vary considerably, however, in the extent to which these various aspects of security are regarded as the responsibility of individuals and their families, and in how far there are expectations that they should be underpinned by state involvement and welfare provisions.

The paradoxes and themes outlined above, then, mean that families are sites of major ambiguities – for both individuals and policymakers – raising the following questions:

- Are families always safe, or are they sometimes very risky and unsafe for individuals?

- Do families 'work' in terms of delivering social order for society more widely, or do they sometimes deliver the opposite?

- Do governments need to intervene to improve the ways in which families 'work' for social order, and to enhance the safety of vulnerable individuals, or do they need to stand back and respect family privacy and the agendas of individual families?

Different social theorists are likely to answer these questions in contrasting ways. But together these questions point, first, to a focus on families and domestic lives in themselves as *sites* of crime in the present (around sexuality, violence and abuse), and, second, to families as *sources* of crime (when they fail to produce stable orderly citizens). Where governments develop policies to respond to such questions, is this a matter of providing welfare support or of controlling social disorder and crime? As you will see in this chapter, even within any one family-based policy initiative that aims to create security both for society and individuals, the balance between welfare/care/support on the one hand, and control/containment/punishment on the other, may shift constantly and ambiguously. This chapter considers how far themes of punitive control and segregation on the one hand, and social protection and preventive partnerships on the other, are tensely interwoven in complex ways in family policies.

Section 2 explores some of the paradoxes of (in)security in family lives, considering variation between families as well as within them. Cultural and historical variations in ideas about childhood and children's needs are the concern of Section 3. This leads, in Section 4, to a particular focus on contemporary anxieties about the nature of childhood, and what it means to be a child or a parent. The section explores the paradoxes of (in)security in contemporary social policies concerned with children's family lives, particularly with regard to the UK Government's 2003 Green Paper *Every Child Matters*, which was the foundation for key policy developments aimed at strengthening preventive services for children in England, prompting much debate about the implications for welfare and control for children, young people and families. Then, using the UK-based examples of residential projects for 'problem families', and the development of Parenting Orders within the criminal justice system, Section 5 explores the question of whether parents are in need of more government and professional support – perhaps generating new anxieties in the process – or whether parents are themselves in need of control and punishment to ensure that families create security for society at large. The relevance of different sorts of evidence to the sensitive issues under discussion is be considered throughout the chapter, with a particular focus on the analysis of policy documents in Section 4, and policy evaluation in Section 5.

2   Paradoxes of (in)secure family lives

If families are seen as the basic building blocks of 'society' and 'social order', it is perhaps not surprising that public and political anxieties about security and risk are often expressed in terms of 'family breakdown'. This draws our attention to the ways in which ideas about 'the family' as a clear-cut, solid-like object have been, and continue to be, embedded in social policies (Fink, 2002), with 'the (nuclear) family' (of the two generational household of two parents living with their biological children) taken to signify 'traditional' stabilities and securities. If 'the family' is 'breaking down', surely this will indeed create insecurity for both individuals and society more generally?

The difficulty with this argument, however, is that it assumes that we all know what is meant by 'the family' and that it can indeed 'exist' as a solid and clear-cut entity in its own right, which can then be seen to be 'breaking down' (or not). Such a view is much easier to hold where we see nuclear families living together in one family home, such that they constitute clearly bounded, co-residential units.

Figure 3.2
The nuclear family can provide an image of a clear residential unit of parents and children

But how are we to understand what 'the family' is, for example, when (biological) parents are living in different households, with children moving between these and relating to a variety of different step- and half-relations? What does 'the family' (or even 'family') mean in these circumstances? Would such a scenario indicate that 'the family' is indeed 'breaking down', or does it indicate that we need to rethink what we might mean by 'family'?

In considering contemporary family lives, there are wide variations in how people describe and evaluate changing patterns. Three main positions can be discerned:

1   Large changes have indeed happened and this is a bad thing (with family breakdown and loss of wider family support causing insecurity and disorder).

2   Large changes have happened and this is a good thing (family changes have freed people to live outside of old restrictions and to develop more individual choice about their lifestyles).

3   There is much continuity as well as change (moral panics about family change are unhelpful and inaccurate – we often repeat the same stories as in the past).

Some major changes certainly seem to be fairly clear in recent decades, including, for example, the rise in births outside marriage, the rise in the numbers of women (including mothers) in formal paid employment, and the rise in single-parent households (Williams, 2004). But even with apparently 'hard' statistics, the 'facts' do not speak for themselves, and much can depend on the way in which we interpret the figures. For example, if we adopt a longer historical time frame, we find that stepfamilies were just as common in the nineteenth century as the late twentieth century in the UK, but historically they resulted from widowhood rather than divorce (Ribbens McCarthy et al., 2003).

Many anthropologists prefer not to use the term 'family' at all, as they suggest it is too closely based on a Western notion of a particular family form (the nuclear family) to be useful in understanding relationships and households in many other cultures. Assumptions about this particular meaning of 'the family' then become the implicit point of comparison for looking at other ways of relating. Furthermore, the ability to privilege certain forms of lifestyle over others – such as the nuclear family household – is itself a powerful form of resource, not least because of the way in which it may present this way of life as somehow 'normal', 'natural', or (somewhat paradoxically) as 'better', or 'healthier'. When such an assumption becomes a form of taken-for-granted 'knowledge' in a given culture, it can be a very powerful way of marginalising, and pathologising, other ways of living. Such processes may be particularly relevant to how we understand the family lives of people who are members of minority ethnic groups. Thus, Phoenix and Husain (2007) have argued that research has tended to position black families in such a way that they tend not to be included in work on 'normal' family lives, but are very visible in research on 'problematic' family lives.

In everyday life, however, even within the UK people vary a great deal in what they mean by 'family', who they would include, and how they feel about this (see, for example, research by Ribbens McCarthy et al., 2003). Some people may think of 'family' in quite a clear-cut way, as the people they live with, and to whom they are related by blood or marriage. Others may have a much looser sense of 'family' as referring to networks of individuals who are spread out across different households, localities or continents. And yet, for each of us, while feelings about our own families may be mixed, our ideas about 'family' may also seem, not only normal, but also natural, correct and proper. So discussion of 'family' is not straightforward: families constitute a contested terrain, and family lives are full of paradoxes and ambiguities, creating dilemmas about how to research them.

Our first key paradox about family, introduced in Section 1, is that families can be sites of *both* security *and* insecurity for individuals. But this is not a matter of some families being 'safe' while others are 'unsafe' – rather, it is a matter of the *same processes* giving rise to variable experiences (of (in)security) such that everyday families are found to be mixed blessings. Thus, the same family practices (Morgan, 1996) that are linked with ideas of safety and nurturance (e.g. care of children or the elderly, provision of resources such as food or warmth) may also give rise to opposite experiences of power struggles, conflict, neglect and abuse. In understanding what is going on in people's lives, then, it is important to recognise that family practices may be ambiguous and that different individuals are likely to experience them in complex and variable ways. Family members themselves may have very different perspectives and understandings about what is occurring in their lives together. Again, from the larger-scale concerns of social policy and professional interventions, there is further scope for viewing family lives and practices through different frameworks and perspectives; for example, as issues of welfare or crime. Thus, the same 'family' activity may be described in different ways, according to the agenda and concerns of the participants or the observer – and again, this can shift almost from moment to moment. So family practices may be reshaped between, and within, welfare and criminal perspectives.

Activity 3.2

Consider some possible family practices involving a father and his 10-year-old son. Examples could be:

■ going to the shops

■ sitting on the settee at home with the TV on

■ driving along in the car.

How do you think the father and the son would each understand what is happening in these activities? In what sense might each activity constitute a 'family practice' implicating (in)security? How might other family members view these practices? How might they be understood in the context of social policies concerned with welfare and crime?

Comment

I will comment briefly on just one activity here, that of sitting on the settee at home with the TV on, which the father may regard as a welcome chance to relax. However, issues of power and control may arise about who selects the TV programme, or issues of discipline and/or conflict if his son disrupts the viewing of the programme. From the son's point of view, this activity may be a chance to share cuddles, talk about the programme, or just enjoy being together. He might have mixed feelings; for example, resenting the programme that's been chosen by his father but enjoying being with him. As observers, then, would we describe this joint activity as a form of fathering?

Figure 3.3
Fathers and sons may
be engaged in various
activities, but what do
they mean in terms of
family practices?

From a social policy point of view, however, we might see other (or different) things going on here. If the father uses unreasonable chastisement to assert his own wishes, we might start to wonder if there are child welfare issues at stake, or at least issues of what constitutes appropriate discipline and parenting style. If there is some apparent interaction and sense of 'togetherness' around watching the TV, we might regard this as the sort of activity that can reduce the chance of children getting into disruptive behaviour outside the home. On the other hand, from the perspective of a health professional, there might be concerns that both father and son are in need of more physical activity, while an educationalist might be concerned whether there is enough verbal or intellectual interaction between father and son to stimulate the boy's cognitive development.

Each description thus frames the activity within a different agenda – one concerning health, education, welfare or crime. But family members may feel that it is no one else's business what they are doing in the privacy of their own home, and social policy debates certainly vary greatly with regard to how we might 'draw the line' around 'private family life'. Issues of welfare and crime constitute important threads in these debates, which takes us to the second paradox identified in Section 1, concerning families as a source of (in)security for society more generally. Welfare policies may suggest a need to intervene in families in order to protect the security of (vulnerable) family members, while concerns with offending behaviours may suggest a need to intervene in families in order to build a secure society. I will consider this further (in Sections 4 and 5) in relation to social policies around parenting and youth offending, but, before pursuing this in any detail, we need to pay attention to the third paradox, introduced in Section 1, concerning the ways in which families may not only create or foster security, but may also themselves be in need of security.

While families are often discussed as somehow rooted in 'nature', we started to consider above how social dimensions are crucial for the ways in which families may vary, both in terms of differences between individual family members, and differences between families. And some patterned social dimensions – including age, gender, ethnicity and class – are likely to be systematically associated with differences of power, and cultural and material resources (see **Newman and Yeates, 2008a**). And yet these, too, are often somehow assumed to be both 'normal' and 'natural' (**Clarke, 2008**), until we look a little further.

By way of illustration, I will consider my own family history. Both my parents were born and raised in terraced houses in North London, with my maternal grandfather being lower middle class (a shop worker), while my father was raised in a skilled working-class household (his foster father was a railway signalman). For both of my parents, the women of the household – including 'spinsters' as well as the married woman of the house – had no regular paid employment outside the home. However, my father was upwardly mobile during his working life, becoming an electrical engineer and a company director, so that I was brought up in a more affluent area, though still very predominantly white and Western European. I remember being aware of social (class) differences between my family and others from a young age, as children from a nearby council estate sometimes mocked my middle-class accent and my clothing. On the other hand, I was also sensitive to other gradations in the social hierarchy when my mother recounted talk between neighbours about who was, or wasn't, from 'the top drawer'; and a school friend was told by her mother that my own family was not really 'suitable' for us to be friends (presumably because we were 'nouveau riche' and thus not from 'the top drawer'). All of these distinctions were associated with differences of housing, locality and other resources, including educational (dis)advantage.

Activity 3.3

Consider how your own experience of 'family' has been affected by class and/or ethnicity, and how this has been manifested at a material level (e.g. through space or time). How far did your parents share their class/ ethnic background? How far were you aware of differences between your class/ethnic background and that of other children's households? How did you become conscious of these differences?

Comment

For families from minority groups, differences centred on ethnicity may be experienced through children's name-calling as well as through some very physical material resources such as housing, as recounted by these interviewees from a study of Caribbean mothers living in England:

> There was this day I picked Malik up from school. He was around five or six years old ... he started crying, saying that these children at his school kept calling him mud-face, and that he's made of mud ... It brought it home that some things don't change, because I was called names, racial names.

> (Tanya, age 40, lone mother, second generation)

> Things were awful in those early days ... We were like aliens from outer space and you could see the fear in their eyes ... I'm sure you heard the stories from your parents about signs landlords used to put in their windows, 'no blacks no dogs and no Irish'.

> (Doris, age 81, married, first generation)
>
> (quoted in Reynolds, 2005, pp. 84 and 71)

Such socially structured differences and inequalities point to questions of how far family members have the resources to provide security for each other. And, as noted in Section 1, where there is a lack of wider security – as with war situations, entrenched poverty, or sectarian violence – it may be almost impossible for family members to provide individuals with basic physical security (some of these issues are returned to in an international context in Chapter 5). In such circumstances, families may be unable to contribute much towards the wider social order.

Within affluent Western societies, some children experience multiple disadvantage or problematic experiences in their lives, which may increase the likelihood of unwelcome experiences later in life. This, then, is a further example relevant to Young's discussion (reviewed in Chapter 1, Section 3) of the ways in which social exclusion may occur (as a result of inequalities of resources) alongside expectations of cultural inclusion – in this case, the widespread assumption that all children should be entitled to a 'normal childhood' in a 'proper family' (Young, 2007). In the remainder of this chapter, then, childhood will be brought into closer view as a particular example of the ways in which paradoxes of (in)security get played out in family lives and social policies.

3   The (in)securities of childhood

Providing for children's needs, with families seen as the primary site for the experience of 'childhood', is another aspect of family lives that may appear to be rooted in nature, through biological processes of

Figure 3.4
Families may not only create or foster security, but may also themselves be in need of security: children of sex workers learning alongside other children in an Indian classroom; a disabled child from a large, inner-city London primary school participating in a race in her wheelchair during a school sports day; young girls sitting together playing handheld video games; a group of child prostitutes on a dusty street in a gold-mining town in Brazil; young children working at their desks in a classroom

(im)maturity. However, ideas about childhood and children's needs vary greatly with economic resources and cultural contexts. Historically, in the context of the urbanisation, industrialisation and economic growth of Western societies over the last two hundred years, ideas developed about 'childhood' as a particular phase of life, ideas which became institutionalised within such policies as child labour legislation and compulsory education.

At the same time, special sites and spaces came to be seen as appropriate places for young people to experience 'childhood', including schools, families and homes. Indeed, families came to be seen as the particular focus for an ethic of care (Fink, 2002), in contrast to the impersonal forces shaping the survival of the strongest in the capitalist markets of the public arena. In such appropriate places, then, children could be both secure and contained, looked after and looked out for, in a complex interweaving of segregation and protection.

Such 'safe' places for children can be contrasted with other spaces which are considered unsuitable for children, including the public spaces of work or the street. Thus, in Westernised expectations, the street may be viewed as an inappropriate place for children, despite the fact that many children in other countries live their entire lives on the street (Boyden, 1990), while 'hanging out' on the street may be felt to be a source of freedom by young people living in both affluent and destitute circumstances (Herrera et al., 2008; Lareau, 2000). Furthermore, Gill (2007) argues that such protection of children may also, paradoxically, increase their vulnerability through restricting their opportunities to learn how to deal with risk in different settings.

Figure 3.5

Is the street incompatible with ideas of 'childhood'?

In many ways, then, notions of childhood in affluent Western societies have led to a view of children as 'different' from adults, vulnerable and dependent, and occupying a special phase of life. Whether or not this 'precious realm' (Parton, 2006, p. 59) is being eroded or extended is, however, heavily debated, with social policies themselves manifesting quite contradictory expectations. So, whilst young people may effectively have been made more legally 'responsible' (accountable for their actions) at an earlier age in relation to crime and wrongdoing in the UK, on the other hand their legal age of attaining adulthood (and thus exiting the special protection of childhood) is potentially being raised in other areas (e.g. buying cigarettes, or obtaining a driving licence), and the duration of youth as a transitional phase is being extended in other aspects of social policy (e.g. minimum wage legislation). Similarly, while parents may complain that young people are 'growing up too fast these days' (particularly through an exposure to mass media and consumerism), on the other hand they may find their offspring remain their resident, financially dependent 'children' well into what might otherwise be considered to be 'adulthood'. Within these various contradictory tendencies, the experience of childhood is under scrutiny, such that 'many of the issues relating to risk and uncertainty can be seen to coalesce around the figure of the child and our anxieties about childhood generally' (Parton, 2006, p. 60).

Such uncertainties concerning the 'nature' of childhood as a social institution contrast quite markedly with perspectives that focus on the particular 'needs' of 'the child', understood to be rooted in biological immaturity. One response of policymakers to the uncertainties over childhood has therefore been to seek more and better evidence about these needs, in order to ensure that children 'develop' appropriately, to become secure and orderly adults. Theories of child development can also be seen to be predominant, even institutionalised, in regulatory social policies such as education, health and welfare (Rose, 1989). Through the focus on the 'needs' of 'the (universal) child', such developmental theories lead into policies and assessments that appear to be based in biology and scientific principles and evidence, even though they are dependent on notions of childhood that are highly culturally and historically variable.

Example

An asylum seeker in the UK has a child who was conceived through rape in her country of origin, who is taken into care due to the mother's mental health problems. Social workers have to assess whether she has bonded with this child, and whether he should be returned to her (in which case, he may get deported with her to her country of origin). Social workers say that she doesn't seem to be paying her child proper attention when she visits him, but she says that in her home country parents don't expect to give children the attention we routinely expect parents to offer here.

Trying to determine the needs of children in practice may, then, pose all sorts of difficulties for the development of appropriate policies across cultural contexts, difficulties which social policies struggle to deal with (as seen, for example, in some of the discussion in the UK Government's Green Paper *Every Child Matters*, which is considered in the next section).

However, while ideas about 'universal' children's needs may appear to be rooted in scientific evidence, they can also carry a strong moral force. Thus, in UK research, people's everyday understandings suggest that children's needs should take priority over those of adults, constituting a moral imperative for those who are seen to be responsible for them – most often, mothers (Ribbens McCarthy et al., 2000). At the same time, children themselves are not held to be morally accountable for their own actions (although this is not to say that they may not exercise all sorts of moral agency and judgements). Part of the reason why children roaming 'loose' outside the home, without adult supervision, sometimes evoke anxiety, is because no one can be held accountable for their actions.

Figure 3.6
Mr Bean let loose in public may cause some anxieties for onlookers

Example

The actor Rowan Atkinson is well known for his role as the catastrophic and socially ineffective 'Mr Bean', who has been the star of several films. In a television interview (*BBC Breakfast*, 30 March 2007), Rowan Atkinson suggested that part of the fascination of Mr Bean is that he behaves like a 10-year-old set loose in public, and travelling the world, with no responsible adult to supervise him or take care of him, or to be held accountable for his disastrous behaviours.

Within such understandings of the responsibilities and accountabilities of adults and children, teenagers seem to occupy a social space that evokes particular anxiety (an issue that is further explored in Chapter 4). As 'adolescents', occupying the social position of 'youth' in which they are in 'transition' between childhood and adulthood, it may be unclear who is to be held accountable for their actions, while at the same time, theories of adolescent development suggest that they have not yet achieved the maturity needed to exercise full moral judgement and responsibility in their own right.

Overall, then, although children may be understood to be in need of security, care and protection, they may also be seen as threats to social order and security if their responsible adults fail to exercise appropriate authority. Children may thus be viewed as both 'at risk' and 'risky'. Furthermore, these increasing anxieties, uncertainties and changing ideas about children's needs and the nature of childhood not only have profound implications for parents, they have also been highly significant for changes in the way social policies and state agencies relate to families. We can explore these tensions through the examples of child protection and surveillance policies, paradoxes of the responsibilisation of parenting – exemplified by the use of residential options for 'problem families'– and the potential juridification of parenting through the introduction of Parenting Orders within the criminal justice system in the UK.

4 Children, parents and government

Anxieties about children are not new, but they run rife through parenting experiences, being embedded in images of children as (vulnerable) 'natural innocents' or as (disruptive) 'little devils' (Ribbens, 1994). But, as I have discussed, the stakes around such tensions have perhaps been raised in recent decades. While changes in family lives in Western societies have heightened fears that 'families' are no longer up to the job, changing ideas about childhood have also seen a proliferation of the needs of the child, to include extensive and increasing nurturing via attention, diet, education, emotional bonding, self-development, etc. If these needs are not met, then children may be identified as being 'at risk' and/or 'risky', but is this a matter of parental protection or discipline, of welfare or control? Indeed, can these different issues be separated out, given the ambiguities of family lives we have been considering?

Activity 3.4

Communication is sometimes discussed as a key element of parenting. How far would you consider talk to be an important feature of parenting teenagers? Why? Do you think that all family members would take a similar view on this?

Comment

The close interconnections between parental care and control can be exemplified through the significance of parents talking to their teenage children. Such talk can be highly ambiguous for both parents and teenagers, raising issues of responsibility, surveillance and control, alongside possibilities of 'openness' and 'closeness' (Gillies et al., 2001). So, while both parents and teenagers may value talk, teenagers may well keep secrets, and parents may sometimes be glad that they do.

Similar ambiguities, around what constitutes care and/or control, can also be seen to occur in social policies and childcare services. In Section 1 of this chapter, I introduced the question of how far it is appropriate for social policies to be developed which intervene in families to enhance security and social order. This is a pervasive question for all governments, although not all governments have the resources to develop extensive policies and services for families. But how far do parents themselves, and their children, experience any particular service provision as 'support' or 'interference', or even 'punishment' (i.e. care or control)? And how far is any particular policy oriented towards protecting children who may be 'at risk' (i.e. a welfare concern directed at ensuring children have the security they need to thrive), or towards controlling children who may be 'risky' (i.e. a control concern directed at ensuring that children do not pose a threat to the security of society at large)? So how far should family policies and services aim to involve all families with children, or to target particular children who are assessed as being especially risky/at risk?

There are no easy answers to such questions, and different welfare regimes and crime control policies will deal with the tensions in different ways. Parton (2006), for example, reviews relevant evidence concerning child protection procedures across a number of Western societies. He suggests a distinction between, on the one hand, a more 'child-saving approach' in which there is a 'legalistically and narrowly defined child protection response', and, on the other hand, a more 'family-service orientation' in which policies are 'generally benign, aimed at helping and providing a more reciprocal and mutually supportive relationship between the state and the family' (Parton, 2006, p. 170). We can see strong resonances between Parton's discussion here and the distinction between state strategies of punitive control or supportive partnerships discussed in Chapter 1 in relation to policies towards security issues generally.

Looking across societies, the evidence suggests that the child-saving approach has historically been predominant in the UK, North America and Australia, while the family-service approach has been more apparent in Northern European and Nordic countries. However, Parton (among others, e.g. see Williams, 2004) argues that, since the 1990s, England has seen a major shift in the relationship between state agencies, parents and children, which represents the most radical approach apparent anywhere in the Western world in its attempt to integrate the two approaches; that is, child protection (through punitive control) and family support (through preventive partnerships). Parton traces these developments to a number of influences, rooted in anxieties about families and childhood. One such influence centres on concerns about social exclusion and the ways in which children who are considered to be 'at risk' may, over time, become 'risky', while various publications argued that we have the research to know what factors can be used to identify such children (although note that how we understand the nature of 'causality' in children's lives over time can be controversial). A second major influence arose from public anxieties about child protection, both in the home (notably through high profile cases of children's deaths through the neglect or violence of their carers) and outside the home (particularly through the perceived threat of predatory paedophiles).

In the UK, these movements underlay the publication of the Green Paper, *Every Child Matters* (DfES, 2003a) and the subsequent Children Act of 2004, which were followed up by other documents, including *Youth Matters* (DfES, 2005), *Youth Matters: Next Steps* (DfES, 2006), *Every Parent*

Matters (DfES, 2007), and, in Scotland, *Getting It Right for Every Child* (Scottish Executive, 2005). These Papers, particularly *Every Child Matters*, provided the basis for extensive changes and developments in services for all families and children.

Activity 3.5

The policies expressed in these Papers were said to be based in the development of new research evidence. However, research evidence comes in many forms, and we can also consider the reports themselves as texts for research analysis in their own right.

Analyses of texts – of many types – constitute an important form of evidence for research into social policy, but this requires that such texts are not taken at face value. Textual sources need careful examination before being taken as evidence, including raising questions about when, how, and why they were written. Public documents – such as a Green Paper – offer a very wide and accessible range of sources, but whose views do they represent, and what may be missing or absent from them? A close attention to the language used in texts can help reveal dominant frames of reference; if the language of policy changes over time, we can legitimately ask what this may signify.

As you read through the following extracts from these reports, try to identify the tensions between:

■ welfare and protection

■ universal and targeted services

■ punitive control and prevention.

How are children and parents described and positioned within these Papers? What notions of 'family' seem to be involved? What are some of the key terms that are used?

Looking through your notes, how would you summarise the principles of the emergent policy framework?

Extract 3.1

Every Child Matters (2003), Introduction by the Chief Secretary to the Treasury

We have to do more both to protect children and ensure each child fulfils their potential. Security and opportunity must go hand in hand. Child protection must be a fundamental element across all public, private and voluntary organisations. Equally, we must be ambitious for all children, whoever they are and wherever they live.

...

... Underpinning this must be not just the resources but an attitude that reflects the value that our society places on children and childhood.

Children are precious. The world they must learn to inhabit is one in which they will face hazards and obstacles alongside real and growing opportunities. They are entitled not just to the sentiment of adults but a strategy that safeguards them as children and realises their potential to the very best of our ability.

Paul Boateng

DfES, 2003a, pp. 3–4

Extract 3.2

Every Child Matters: Summary (2003)

We need to ensure we properly protect children at risk within a framework of universal services which support every child to develop their full potential and which aim to prevent negative outcomes. That is why this Green Paper addressed the needs of children at risk in the context of services we provide for all children.

...

Where we want to get to

Our aim is to ensure that every child has the chance to fulfil their potential by reducing levels of educational failure, ill health, substance misuse, teenage pregnancy, abuse and neglect, crime and anti-social behaviour among children and young people.

When we consulted children, young people and families, they wanted the Government to set out a positive vision of the outcomes we want to achieve. The five outcomes which mattered most to children and young people were:

- *being healthy:* enjoying good physical and mental health and living a healthy lifestyle

- *staying safe:* being protected from harm and neglect

- *enjoying and achieving:* getting the most out of life and developing the skills for adulthood

- *making a positive contribution:* being involved with the community and society and not engaging in anti-social or offending behaviour

- *economic well-being:* not being prevented by economic disadvantage from achieving their full potential in life.

...

Supporting parents and carers

The Government intends to put supporting parents and carers at the heart of its approach to improving children's lives, where support is needed or wanted. ... We are consulting on a long-term vision to improve parenting and family support through:

- *universal services* such as schools, health and social services and childcare, providing information and advice and engaging parents to support their children's development

- *targeted and specialist support* to parents of children requiring additional support

- *compulsory action* through Parenting Orders as a last resort where parents are condoning a child's truancy, anti-social behaviour or offending.

DfES, 2003b, pp. 5, 7, 9

Extract 3.3

Every Parent Matters (2007)

While seeking to create the conditions within which many more parents themselves feel confident about engaging effectively with their children's learning and development, government must pay particular attention to parents, for whatever reason, who currently lack the motivation, skills or awareness to do so. ...

...

That said, for a small minority of parents who have lost, or never had, the capacity to parent responsibly, public services must be ready to intervene promptly and sensitively. Parents in this situation may be distressed by being unable to resolve their problems alone and afraid of being seen as failures. The ultimate objective remains to enable them confidently to raise their children effectively themselves. However, we have to accept that this journey may be a long one and compulsion for the few, through measures such as parenting orders, may sometimes be required to ensure that responsibilities to the child (such as getting them to school every day) are being properly fulfilled.

...

Most parents take seriously their responsibilities to ensure that their child attends school and behaves appropriately – whether in school or in the wider community. Some parents need help to do this effectively and this can be provided by way of a parenting contract or through other, less formal, means. But the small number of parents unwilling to accept help and fulfil their responsibilities must be compelled to do so.

...

Parents that will not act to improve their child's attendance or behaviour can be made subject to a court-imposed parenting order. This compels the parent to attend parenting classes and comply with any other conditions set out in the order. Currently, only local authorities can be granted such orders but, from September 2007, schools will be able to apply for such orders where a pupil has seriously misbehaved or been excluded for serious misbehaviour.

DfES, 2007, pp. 6, 7, 26, 27

Comment

The discussion below will explore more fully some of the issues and implications of these reports. While a full textual analysis of these (heavily selected) extracts would require a more extensive research report, my initial thoughts suggest that there is an overwhelming language of 'supporting' parents, who are said to be heavily responsible for their children's 'outcomes'. 'Precious' children are 'entitled' to goods such as: safety, security, protection, '[to] support every child to develop their full potential and ... prevent negative outcomes'. Parents, on the other hand, are discussed by reference to responsibilities rather than entitlements, and are thus expected to fulfil their responsibilities to their children, to (voluntarily?) access support, become involved with services, and make choices, 'engaging effectively with their children's learning and development'. Indeed, one might see this as amounting to enforced responsibilisation for parents, since parents who do not voluntarily pursue their responsibilities may be obliged to do so. Thus, closely interwoven with this emphasis on universal support is a concern with antisocial and truanting behaviour, discussed within a framework of wanting to maximise children's potential, but leading into an expressed need to target unmotivated parents, or those who lack the capacity to parent effectively, and invoking compulsion 'as a last resort' for parents who, 'for whatever reason ... currently lack the motivation, skills or awareness' or 'have lost, or never had, the capacity to parent responsibly'. Some parents are thus described as 'condoning' certain behaviours, and lacking in motivation or capacity.

Overall, then, all parents – but particularly those from more disadvantaged or minority backgrounds – may feel they are under greatly increased scrutiny and surveillance, to show that they are engaging with services and fulfilling their responsibilities for their children. But within the Green Papers, what sorts of families are assumed, and who exactly counts as 'parent', is not explicitly discussed. While some sections of *Every Parent Matters* specifically discuss the importance of fathers, as you will see in Section 5, it tends to be overwhelmingly women who become involved in these processes of surveillance and monitoring. What starts with a concern with child protection thus moves into surveillance processes that involve all 'families' but may or may not, or perhaps may only very ambiguously, be experienced as supportive. As a result of these measures, then, Parton (2006) suggests that a social investment model of the 'preventive' welfare state was to be delivered through a three-pronged approach, including: general support for all parents with children; targeted support for poor families with children; and specific policies for children considered to be 'at risk'.

Furthermore, this shift of focus, away from specific groups of children towards policies concerning all children, was to be underpinned by a new drive towards the sharing of information between professionals across various agencies, through the establishment of a national database on children. But should these developments be understood as the state investing in children's futures, or intervening in family lives? It is here that the tensions involved in combining a concern with commitment to a family-service orientation with child protection become most apparent, since the focus on protection and prevention leads into a general policy of surveillance, and thus potentially interference, which is hard to reconcile in any simple way with an orientation to benign, mutual support between parents and government, towards the welfare of children.

At the same time, themes of child protection coexist uneasily with newer ideas about children's rights, pointing to key paradoxes for parents. So, should families be understood as democracies (Giddens, 1992), involving children as small people who have rights to be heard, *or* as authoritative units whose job it is to uphold proper values, involving children who need protection via care and control? What are parents going to make of these tensions?

> **Example**
>
> A young, white, working-class mother – who already felt devalued for being a teenage mother – first attended some counselling sessions arranged by her doctor, and later attended parenting classes provided through her local health centre after moving house. In the counselling sessions she felt judged and intimidated, and that her parenting was inadequate. In the parenting classes she felt supported and encouraged, and that she could develop new parenting ideas that resonated with her own existing ideas. This included thinking about how to let her children make their own decisions and take their own responsibilities as they got older. But this then led her to question, and refuse to sign, the home–school agreement that her older children brought home from school.

Tensions in social policies thus get translated into tensions in parents' daily experiences, as parents deal with conflicting ideas about how far they are (and should be) responsible for their children's behaviour, particularly in relation to teenagers.

There has thus been an increasing focus on parenting itself, with research seeking to identify the factors thought to promote children's welfare, and preventing them from being at risk/risky. Some of these factors include resource issues such as poverty, disability, or poor housing, but not all parents and children living in disadvantaged circumstances are necessarily at risk/risky, which has also led to research interest in how parenting occurs in contexts of poverty and disadvantage (Hooper et al., 2007). Parenting 'practices' themselves have thus come under scrutiny, with 'poor parenting' identified as a major factor in children's disorderliness and later offending behaviours (Parton, 2006).

A mixture of more targeted policies has thus been developed alongside more universal services to intervene in such issues, but whether such policies are experienced as supportive or regulatory by parents and children themselves may provoke much debate, requiring sensitive analysis of the research evidence. Two examples, relevant to our present discussion, are considered in the next section: residential options for 'problem families', and Parenting Orders.

5 Targeting 'irresponsible' parents: assessing the evidence

5.1 Residential support

The Dundee Families Project is a residential option for families which has received considerable attention from politicians and researchers. It was established in 1996 to provide special accommodation and/or intensive support to families (mostly mothers and children) identified as being either homeless or at very real risk of homelessness as a consequence of antisocial behaviour. It has been described as 'pioneering' and taken as a model for the expansion of similar services elsewhere (DfES, 2007). Garrett (2007) points out that such residential options have quite a long history (both in the UK and elsewhere) in policies attempting to turn 'weak' or 'asocial' families into productive members of society, and he reviews evidence evaluating the effectiveness of the Dundee project specifically. Many of the families involved were experiencing high levels of poverty, ill health, mental health problems, and child abuse, and were often *themselves* the victims of harassment. One study suggested that the experiences of those living in the project accommodation were very mixed, and at times ambivalent:

> Although living in core accommodation brings with it restrictions on freedom, paradoxically, this enabled some families more freedom than they experienced previously. In some cases families had previously lived within environments characterised by risk, vulnerability and volatility and as a consequence, living in core accommodation enabled service users to feel safe.
>
> (Nixon et al., 2006, quoted in Garrett, 2007, p. 220)

On the other hand, research by Dillane et al. (2001) suggested that the services operated on a mixture of 'persuasion and coercion' (quoted in Garrett, 2007, p. 214), with some families experiencing an unexpected scrutiny of their personal relationships. Garrett (2007, p. 221) thus suggests that many families had been 'coerced and hoodwinked' at the point of referral into these projects, and that the dominant approach of containment and surveillance had the effect of infantilising adults – concerns which he suggests were glossed over in the evaluation reports. This raises major issues about the role of evidence in evaluating social policies, and how researchers interpret the tensions and ambiguities involved in complex social processes.

5.2 The impact of Parenting Orders

Similar issues of how to interpret the evaluation research evidence arise in relation to other more widely used parenting policy initiatives. Thus parenting classes may also carry major ambiguities in terms of whether they are experienced as supportive, regulatory or punitive. A particularly controversial feature within the UK has been the provision of such 'support' (via Parenting Orders) within the framework of the criminal justice system, effectively a process of juridification of parenting. Such policies highlight policy tensions around whether, and how, youth justice provisions should be integrated with other children's services.

Ghate and Ramella (2002) carried out a major study to evaluate the effectiveness of such Orders, gathering information from workers and families throughout the UK. They found some evidence that parents experienced parenting classes as helpful and useful even within the Parenting Orders framework, and that parents, who otherwise would be very hard to engage with, were being brought into services. Nevertheless, it also appeared that considerable effort first had to be made to reassure parents (through intensive one-to-one engagement) that the classes were not going to 'blame' or judge them. While Ghate and Ramella were thus concerned to highlight the benefits experienced by some severely disadvantaged mothers (with high levels of need) within this framework, their evaluation was based on the small minority of parents who participated in the programme and were prepared to complete evaluation questionnaires. Their evaluation of the projects was also undermined by the absence of any control groups (i.e. groups of other similar parents who could be compared over the same time frame but who did not experience Parenting Orders). We also have no means of knowing how far these benefits were sustained after the conclusion of the six- to eight-week programmes, after which parents were simply left to manage alone again.

Parenting Orders have also been strongly criticised (e.g. by Goldson and Jamieson, 2002) for framing and resourcing the interventions that parents receive within a criminal justice system that risks being seen as punitive. This may be partly a matter of available resources, but it may also occur because governments want to be seen to be acting in response to criminal behaviours. While Arthur (2005) suggests that evidence strongly supports the view that parenting is a key issue for juvenile offending (though note that there are complex issues at stake in inferring such causal relationships), he also argues that 'poor parenting' is closely linked to social and economic deprivation, so it is actually counterproductive to treat parents punitively in relation to their young offenders, when these 'damaged and damaging' families really need support and parenting education set within a welfare framework.

Another key feature of the evaluation research of Parenting Orders by Ghate and Ramella was that they largely found that white working-class families (particularly mothers and sons) were involved in the projects. Consequently, we know very little about how parents from minority ethnic groups might experience such Orders. This points to related cultural issues about what is 'good' or appropriate parenting (across class as well as ethnic cultures), and what may constitute 'normal' child development. Understanding our own cultural assumptions, and being able to deal with the diversity of family lives across – and within – a wide variety of different contexts, may require very skilled and sensitive listening skills and research (e.g. see Reynolds and Zontini, 2006).

6 Review

In this chapter you have looked at the ways in which families are understood as:

- key sets of social relationships in which individuals may experience and develop a sense of safety or vulnerability, security or risk

- key sites for the successful production of social order through stable and productive citizenship, or for the failure to contain disorder, with antisocial and criminal behaviours as the consequence.

You have seen how 'family' is understood as the primary social unit which binds individuals into society, but often imbued with norms and ideals in ways that obscure the power dimensions at stake, especially around gender and generation. Such idealised, culturally and historically based understandings of 'family' and 'childhood' may need to be uncovered and sensitively analysed before we can understand how these issues are played out in the complexities of everyday family and social policy practices.

Changing families and related social policies may be subject to varied evaluations. These range from a pessimistic concern with family life as 'breaking down' as a result of women's expectations of equality within and outside the home, to a more optimistic sense of relief at the long-overdue recognition of injustices, such as child sexual abuse in families and the need for appropriate responses from the criminal justice system. Arguably, the potential for abuse and violence within families has in some respects become more fully recognised in Western societies since the latter part of the twentieth century, and social policies may thus be oriented *both* to the protection of individuals *within* families and the protection of society *from* the failures of family, as a social unit, to produce social order.

There is also a risk, however, that such policies – in the drive to ensure we have families that *create* security – may overlook the ways in which families themselves may be *in need* of security, in terms of both economic and social resources. But different theoretical, research and policy approaches vary in whether, and how, they focus on individuals, families or wider social structures.

Such tensions and paradoxes lead to complex ambiguities about what constitutes support, intervention, control and punishment in family contexts, and these tensions are also highly apparent in the use of research evidence. This chapter has drawn to varying degrees on a range of evidence, including:

■ statistical trends over time concerning family change

■ surveys that seek to identify causal factors underlying particular childhood 'outcomes'

■ comparative analyses of social policies across different societies

■ textual analysis of policy documents, particularly relating to *Every Child Matters*

■ evaluation research concerning specific policy provisions, particularly residential provisions for 'problem families' (sometimes referred to as 'sinbins') and compulsory participation in parenting classes in conjunction with Parenting Orders.

All of these point, in different ways, to major issues of how to assess the adequacy of the research, and, even more difficult, how to capture and interpret the ambiguities of complex interactions around family lives.

In this chapter, I have focused in particular on uncertainties about childhood, and the significance attached to children as the future of society, in order to consider how the entanglements of crime and welfare in the pursuit of security can be seen to be particularly closely intertwined in the context of family lives. Key dilemmas for governments concern how far to intervene in family lives, and whether services should be universal or targeted. And while universal services may be considered less stigmatising, they may also shift the delicate balance around what is considered to be appropriate in terms of government involvement in family lives. Several writers thus argue that an increased concern with security has led to a significant shift in this balance in twenty-first-century Western societies. As a result, it appears that we have seen an extension of policies that are explicitly oriented towards developing a new consensus around what leads to security in family lives and relationships, along with the criminalisation and punishment of those who depart from these expectations. Some of these issues – of the extension of the criminal justice system and the regulation of social lives – are explored further in the next chapter.

Further reading

Early twenty-first-century developments in childcare polices are thoroughly reviewed by Nigel Parton in *Safeguarding Childhood: Early Intervention and Surveillance in a Late Modern Society* (2006, Palgrave Macmillan). He considers the ways in which the relationship between child protection and support for families has shaped contemporary social policy in the context of changing social attitudes. Fiona Williams's *Rethinking Families* (2004, Calouste Gulbenkian Foundation) provides a helpful, evidence-based overview of family changes and policies, from a UK perspective.

References

Arthur, R. (2005) 'Punishing parents for the crimes of their children', *Howard Journal*, vol. 44, no. 3, pp. 233–53.

Boyden, J. (1990) 'Childhood and the policy makers: a comparative perspective on the globalisation of childhood' in James, A. and Prout, A. (eds) (1990) *Constructing and Reconstructing Childhood: Contemporary Issues in the Sociological Study of Childhood*, Lewes, Falmer.

Clarke, J. (2008) 'Looking for social justice: welfare states and beyond' in Newman and Yeates (eds) (2008b).

Department for Education and Skills (DfES)(2003a) *Every Child Matters*, Cm 5860, Norwich, The Stationery Office; also available online at http://publications.everychildmatters.gov.uk/eOrderingDownload/CM5860.pdf (Accessed 9 January 2008).

Department for Education and Skills (DfES) (2003b) *Every Child Matters: Summary*, Nottingham, DfES Publications; also available online at http://www.everychildmatters.gov.uk/_files/ B889EFF62F56A9E4C69778A869B3DA44.pdf (Accessed 8 January 2008).

Department for Education and Skills (DfES) (2005) *Youth Matters*, Cm 6629, Norwich, The Stationery Office; also available online at http://www.dfes.gov.uk/ consultations/downloadableDocs/Youth%20mattters%20pdf.pdf (Accessed 10 January 2008).

Department for Education and Skills (DfES) (2006) *Youth Matters: Next Steps*, Nottingham, DfES Publications; also available online at http://www.dfes.gov.uk/ publications/youth/downloads.shtml (Accessed 10 January 2008).

Department for Education and Skills (DfES) (2007) *Every Parent Matters*, Nottingham, DfES Publications; also available online at http://www.teachernet.gov.uk/_doc/11184/ 6937_DFES_Every_Parent_Matters_FINAL_PDF_as_published_130307.pdf (Accessed 10 January 2008).

Fink, J. (2002) 'Private lives, public issues: moral panics and "the family" in 20th-century Britain', *Journal for the Study of British Cultures*, vol. 9, no. 2, pp. 135–48.

Garrett, P.M. (2007) '"Sinbin" solutions: the "pioneer" projects for "problem families" and the forgetfulness of social policy research', *Critical Social Policy*, vol. 27, no. 2, pp. 203–30.

Ghate, D. and Ramella, M. (2002) *The National Evaluation of the Youth Justice Board's Parenting Programme*, London, Policy Research Bureau.

Giddens, A. (1992) *The Transformation of Intimacy: Sexuality, Love and Eroticism in Modern Societies*, Cambridge, Polity Press.

Gill, T. (2007) *No Fear: Growing Up in a Risk Averse Society*, London, Calouste Gulbenkian Foundation.

Gillies, V., Ribbens McCarthy, J. and Holland, J. (2001) *Pulling Together, Pulling Apart: The Family Lives of 16–18 Year Olds,* London, Family Policy Studies Centre/ Joseph Rowntree Foundation.

Goldson, B. and Jamieson, J. (2002) 'Youth crime, the "parenting deficit" and state intervention: a contextual critique', *Youth Justice*, vol. 2, no. 2, pp. 82–99.

Herrera, E., Jones, G. and Thomas de Benitez, S. (2008) 'Bodies on the line: identity markers among Mexican street youth', *Children's Geographies* (forthcoming).

Hooper, C.-A., Gorin, S., Cabral, C. and Dyson, C. (2007) *Living with Hardship 24/7: The Diverse Experiences of Families in Poverty in England*, London, The Frank Buttle Trust.

Lareau, A. (2000) 'Social class and the daily lives of children: a study from the United States', *Childhood*, vol. 7, no. 2, pp. 155–71.

Mooney, G. and Neal, S. (eds) (2009) *Community: Welfare, Crime and Society*, Maidenhead, Open University Press/Milton Keynes, The Open University.

Morgan, D.H.J. (1996) *Family Connections: An Introduction to Family Studies*, Cambridge, Polity Press.

Newman, J. and Yeates, N. (2008a) 'Making social justice: ideas, struggles and responses' in Newman and Yeates (eds) (2008b).

Newman, J. and Yeates, N. (eds) (2008b) *Social Justice: Welfare, Crime and Society*, Maidenhead, Open University Press/Milton Keynes, The Open University.

Parton, N. (2006) *Safeguarding Childhood: Early Intervention and Surveillance in a Late Modern Society*, Basingstoke, Palgrave Macmillan.

Phoenix, A. and Husain, F. (2007) *Parenting and Ethnicity*, York, Joseph Rowntree Foundation/National Children's Bureau.

Reynolds, T. (2005) *Caribbean Mothers: Identity and Experience in the UK*, London, Tufnell Press.

Reynolds, T. and Zontini, E. (2006) *Families, Social Capital and Ethnic Identities of Caribbeans, South Asians and South Europeans*, London, London South Bank University.

Ribbens, J. (1994) *Mothers and Their Children: A Sociology of Childrearing*, London, Sage.

Ribbens McCarthy, J., Edwards, R. and Gillies, V. (2000) 'Moral tales of the child and the adult: narratives of contemporary family lives under changing circumstances', *Sociology*, vol. 34, no. 4, pp. 785–804.

Ribbens McCarthy, J., Edwards, R. and Gillies, V. (2003) *Making Families: Moral Tales of Parenting and Step-Parenting*, Durham, Sociology Press.

Rose, N. (1989) *Governing the Soul: The Shaping of the Private Self*, London, Routledge.

Scottish Executive (2005) *Getting It Right For Every Child* [online], http://childpolicyinfo.childreninscotland.org.uk/index/news-app?story=3841 (Accessed 27 October 2007).

Williams, F. (2004) *Rethinking Families*, London, Calouste Gulbenkian Foundation.

Young, J. (2007) *The Vertigo of Late Modernity*, London, Sage.

Chapter 4
Criminalising conduct

Ross Fergusson and John Muncie

Contents

1   Introduction

The discussion of families in the previous chapter has highlighted ways in which support for those facing particular difficulties often takes the form of disciplinary intervention. The search for security involves the classification of particular forms of behaviour as problematic (and potentially threatening), which may in turn be identified as targets of public policy.

In this context, discourses around crime and the fear of crime have centred on identifying a range of troubled and troubling conduct which, *if it were generalised*, might undermine the norms of behaviour that are thought fundamental to security. In this chapter we will explore two forms of conduct that are perceived in this way. The first concerns what has become defined as 'antisocial behaviour', the second concerns what are termed 'hate crimes'. Both exist in a grey area of what is considered 'undesirable' but has not until recently been subject to criminal law. Behaviour driven by incivility or nuisance, and by hate or prejudice is difficult to define for the purposes of criminal sanction. Nevertheless, both have been legislated against since the 1980s in the UK and the USA, albeit in different ways. Both imply the replacement of private and social loyalties and obligations by contractual or formal legal ones. In the case of antisocial behaviour, this results from a breakdown in informal controls in the community; while in the case of hate crime, it arises from a breakdown in tolerance and from difficulties in handling difference.

The pressure to legislate against hate and incivility suggests not only that such behaviours are becoming more prevalent but also that they are indicative of a major breakdown in 'normal social relations' whereby 'tolerance of difference' has been supplanted by 'fear of the stranger'. *The study of hate and antisocial behaviour legislation allows us to test the thesis that there is a growing tendency to abandon a welfarist ethos of tolerance, support and protection in favour of formal and coercive criminal justice interventions (identified as punitiveness in Chapter 1).*

However they are defined and dealt with, all the forms of conduct explored in this chapter are concerned with the complex, shifting and sometimes contradictory ways in which behaviour is influenced, shaped, guided and regulated by other people or agencies.

The aims of this chapter are to:

- consider the impact of legislation around antisocial behaviour and hate crime with the help of the concepts of juridification and criminalisation

- consider whether the juridification and criminalisation of conduct are part of a move towards a less tolerant society

■ consider what evidence would be required to substantiate such a view

■ explore the ways in which the criminalisation of conduct reflects the entanglement of social welfare and crime control

■ explore alternatives to using the criminal law as the key means to resolve conflict.

Section 2 traces the evolution of legislation about antisocial behaviour in the UK from concerns about 'unruly tenants' to those about 'feral youth'. One way of making sense of this shift is through the concepts of *juridification* and *criminalisation* which are explored in Section 2.2. These concepts are then tested in Section 3 by examining legislation directed against prejudice through anti-discrimination law in the 1980s and hate crime law since 2000. Section 4 highlights the importance of evidence by considering difficulties of finding clear, reliable statistical measures of antisocial behaviour and hate. Section 5 subjects the concept of juridification to critical enquiry, by returning to the theories of prevention and responsibilisation that were introduced in Chapter 1, and by introducing alternative forms of 'restorative' justice that depend less on formal criminal law.

2   Identifying antisocial behaviour

Activity 4.1

Make a brief note of troublesome behaviours which you regard as undesirable, annoying or intimidating in your local area. Rank them in terms of their seriousness and frequency and who are most likely to be their perpetrators.

Now make a quick categorisation of each as one of the following:

■ behaviours you simply find annoying

■ behaviours you think might be labelled 'antisocial'

■ behaviours which are criminal.

Next, try to label each behaviour as one of the following:

■ a 'pet hate' of your own

■ a widely perceived nuisance

■ a threat to the well-being of other citizens.

Now label each one as:

■ occurring rarely

■ increasingly common

- part of a 'trend'
- prevalent over a long time

... and as predominantly committed by:

- children
- adolescents
- young adults
- middle-aged people
- pensioners.

Look over your list to see if you can identify any patterns or connections in the ways you have classified the behaviours. Are minor nuisances or annoying behaviours also the most common and least serious in terms of threats to well-being? Are unlawful behaviours also the most serious and the least common? And so on.

Comment

It will be clear that defining the concept of antisocial behaviour is difficult and subjective. Behaviours may also be regarded as antisocial (or not) depending on the incidence, the context in which they occur, whose behaviour is in question, and at whom the behaviour is directed. Even with the option to construct your own definitions, you will probably have found it difficult to categorise all of the behaviours. It would be quite unusual if you had put together tidy bundles in which there was a simple correspondence between your initial label (nuisance, criminal, etc.) and the seriousness and incidence of the behaviour. The exception might be with regard to which groups of people are seen to perpetrate antisocial behaviour: typically, troublesome behaviour is most widely associated with young people.

Activity 4.2

Look at the typology and categorisations of antisocial behaviour listed in Table 4.1 (taken from the Home Office document *Defining and Measuring Anti-social Behaviour*) and make notes in answer to these questions:

- Which antisocial behaviours do you consider more of an annoyance than personally threatening?
- Which behaviours do you think are a 'physical threat' to your personal security?
- Which are serious enough to warrant criminal sanction?
- Is there any common theme that connects these behaviours?

Table 4.1 Home Office typology of antisocial behaviour

Misuse of public space	Disregard for community/ personal well-being	Acts directed at people	Environmental damage
Drug/substance misuse and dealing Taking drugs Sniffing volatile substances Discarding needles/ drug paraphernalia Crack houses Presence of dealers or users **Street drinking** **Begging** **Prostitution** Soliciting Cards in phone boxes Discarded condoms **Kerb crawling** Loitering Pestering residents **Sexual acts** Inappropriate sexual conduct Indecent exposure **Abandoned cars** **Vehicle-related nuisance & inappropriate vehicle use** Inconvenient/illegal parking Car repairs on the street/in gardens Setting vehicles alight Joyriding Racing cars Off-road motorcycling Cycling/skateboarding in pedestrian areas/ footpaths	**Noise** Noisy neighbours Noisy cars/motorbikes Loud music Alarms (persistent ringing/ malfunction) Noise from pubs/clubs Noise from business/ industry **Rowdy behaviour** Shouting & swearing Fighting Drunken behaviour Hooliganism/loutish behaviour **Nuisance behaviour** Urinating in public Setting fires (not directed at specific persons or property) Inappropriate use of fireworks Throwing missiles Climbing on buildings Impeding access to communal areas Games in restricted/ inappropriate areas Misuse of air guns Letting down tyres **Hoax calls** False calls to emergency services **Animal-related problems** Uncontrolled animals	**Intimidation/ harassment** Groups or individuals making threats Verbal abuse Bullying Following people Pestering people Voyeurism Sending nasty/ offensive letters Obscene/ nuisance phone calls Menacing gestures *Can be on the grounds of:* Race Sexual orientation Gender Religion Disability Age	**Criminal damage/ vandalism** Graffiti Damage to bus shelters Damage to phone kiosks Damage to street furniture Damage to buildings Damage to trees/plants/ hedges **Litter/rubbish** Dropping litter Dumping rubbish Fly-tipping Fly-posting

Source: Harradine et al., 2004, p. 4, Table 2.1

Comment

Some of these behaviours pose a material threat to the *security* of some people. Most of the vehicle-related behaviours could easily result in injury to third parties. So also could setting fires, inappropriate use of fireworks, throwing missiles, misuse of air guns, and uncontrolled animals. In extreme cases, false calls to emergency services pose a threat to the well-being of someone needing them. But most of the behaviours are not direct threats to the security of any *specific* person. If they were, they would already be the subject of legislation against assault, threatening behaviour or criminal damage. Rather, these are for the most part *generalised* problem behaviours, characterised by:

■ their *potential* to harm a specific person or property

■ their *undirected* nature, with regard to people or property

■ the *implied* threat that derives from their *association* with offensive or harmful behaviour

■ the threat they would pose *if* they were directed at a particular person or their property.

Figure 4.1
Celebrating the antisocial? A Eurostar advertisement in Brussels designed to attract visitors to England

However troublesome antisocial behaviour might be, very little of it is a direct threat to our material security. Rather, it is a reminder of perceptions of a whole range of behaviours that *might* compromise our

security at some future unspecified date. It is in large part about how we *feel* when we are reminded of people who are addicted to classified drugs, who live by hiring out their bodies for sex, or who live on the street. However little they threaten our material security, they seem to increase our sense of vulnerability. Much of this and the associations on which it depends are themselves products of these social processes. Importantly too, many of the behaviours that evoke fear might in other contexts evoke sympathy or a desire to help someone who is poor or vulnerable.

2.1 Ordering lives: young people and antisocial behaviour

The strong association between the activities in Table 4.1 and the behaviours of young people needs no elaboration. The activities listed under 'disregard for community/personal well-being' and 'environmental damage' catalogue stereotypical youthful misdemeanours. So the focus here will be on young people, partly because of their prominence in perceived antisocial behaviour, but also partly because the ways in which their misconduct is treated *highlights significant dilemmas and contradictions between welfare and crime control.*

Activity 4.3

Consider the following three cases and think about whether the Anti-social Behaviour Orders imposed might pose difficulties or if they seem likely to prevent the 'offence' occurring.

1   In 1999, a 14-year-old boy in Nottingham, previously convicted for theft, robbery and racial harassment, was ordered to stay away from all properties within three-quarters of a mile of his home and to stop using abusive and threatening language within the same radius. The order was imposed for two years with the sanction that failure to comply might lead to a prison sentence.

2   In County Durham, a 15-year-old was given an Anti-social Behaviour Order banning him from playing football in the street after having twelve footballs confiscated in two weeks.

3   A 14-year-old in Manchester was banned from putting his hood up except in bad weather, under an interim Anti-social Behaviour Order, on the basis that 'his face should be seen and not hidden'.

Comment

These cases draw attention to the difficulties and contradictions of bringing the force of law to bear upon minor or nuisance 'misconduct'. In the first case, these provisions would be very difficult to police, as they would require constant surveillance. In the second case, there is nothing to stop the behaviour from simply being transferred to another place. The Order imposed in the third case seems absurd, in that it focuses entirely on the positioning of an item of clothing. In all three cases, nothing was put into place to address the causes of the behaviour.

While official concern over youthful 'delinquency' can be traced in the UK to the 1816 *Report of the Society for Investigating the Causes of the Alarming Increase of Juvenile Delinquency in the Metropolis* (Muncie, 2004), the term 'antisocial behaviour' has rapidly risen to prominence since the 1990s and has been particularly directed at the misbehaviour of young people. In other countries, such as the USA, where similar concerns have been expressed, legislation has been more targeted – for example, by imposing injunctions against gangs – while in the UK it has become inextricably bound up with the politics of crime and disorder (Squires, 2006). One of the first official publications was the consultation paper *A Quiet Life: Tough Action on Criminal Neighbours* published in 1995 (Labour Party, 1995). Here, the issue was initially constructed in terms of 'neighbours from hell'; the document demanded legislative action on housing management and called for stronger powers against troublesome tenants (Burney, 2005). By 1997 the UK Government proposed new legislative powers for dealing with social housing tenants, the Community Safety Order (later to be renamed as the Anti-social Behaviour Order, or ASBO) which was directed at what was then termed 'antisocial *criminal* behaviour'.

Subsequently, antisocial behaviour became almost synonymous with youth disorder, particularly in 'high crime/sink estates'. Partially justified as welfare protection, the White Paper *No More Excuses: A New Approach to Tackling Youth Crime in England and Wales* (Home Office, 1997) outlined an expanded youth justice apparatus that would embrace a widening population of children and their parents through *pre-emptive interventions*. A range of provisions was proposed that would enable antisocial acts to be prosecuted more efficiently, ensure parents took responsibility for their children's behaviour, and target for *early intervention* those deemed 'at risk' (see Chapter 3). Notably, this strategy represented a shift away from traditional attempts to address children's offending through notions of child protection and universal welfare needs (Muncie, 2004). The emergent strategy was formalised in the 1998 Crime and Disorder Act which prioritised the principle of *preventing* offending by children and young people.

These were hugely significant developments that redrew the boundaries between social policy and crime control, and ultimately between welfare and punishment. On the one hand, the new approach to youth crime proposed legislation in an area in which the law was not previously thought to be a necessary, appropriate or effective means of intervention; on the other, it aimed to find new ways of protecting the well-being of particular groups of young people. Reducing welfare provision as a right for all citizens regardless of their means and their needs was a fundamental feature of radical changes in government policy through the 1980s and 1990s (see **Clarke, 2008** and Chapter 1 in this volume). Concerned at the neglect of the needs of some 'excluded' groups of young people, policies targeted welfare interventions where they were considered to be most needed, replacing universal provision. Successful targeting entailed making judgements about whose need was greatest before it became apparent and the 'damage was done'. This gave rise to risk assessments, mostly based on place of residence and parents' income (see Chapters 1 and 3). Pre-empting antisocial behaviour, anticipating risk, preventing offending, and targeted interventions were at the heart of these strategies.

Figure 4.2
Merseyside Police Community Support Officers in St Helens have been given digital cameras to capture evidence of antisocial behaviour such as graffiti, criminal damage and fly-tipping

This approach to dealing with 'risky' and 'at risk' youth was given further weight in the Anti-social Behaviour Act 2003 which introduced more enforcement-led interventions, including Parenting Contracts, Fixed Penalty Notices and Dispersal Orders. The latter operate in designated dispersal zones when authorised by the local authority and the police on the basis that a member of the public *might be* 'intimidated, harassed, alarmed or distressed'. If two or more people, together in a public place, fail to disperse under the instruction of a police officer, they have committed a criminal offence and face possible detention. Unaccompanied under-16-year-olds can be escorted home by the police. Significantly, the Act also granted groups other than the police, including private security guards, the power to issue fines. The Serious Organised Crime and Police Act 2005 removed legal safeguards protecting the anonymity of children who breached the terms of their ASBO so that they could be publicly 'named and shamed'.

The concept of responsibilisation examined in Chapter 1 is relevant here. Parents could be held to account if their children misbehaved, and could be subject to fines or Parenting Orders, predicated on the assumption that they were implicated in their child's behaviour (see Chapter 3). But how far does the principle of prevention – whereby the criminal justice system attempted to predict who might be disposed towards committing criminal behaviour – make the *apparent* intention itself an offence? A number of precedents were set at this time, while other long-protected principles were breached:

■ Some forms of social misconduct were made statutory offences.

■ People who had not themselves committed an offence (parents) could be held legally responsible for people who had done so (their children aged up to 16), and were made eligible for prosecution.

■ While antisocial behaviour was established as an offence in civil law, failure to comply with an ASBO was made a criminal offence subject to custodial sentence.

By 2006, 6500 ASBOs, 13,000 Acceptable Behaviour Contracts, 800 Dispersal Orders and almost 200,000 Penalty Notices for Disorder had been issued (10 Downing Street, 2006). But the first major independent study into the use of ASBOs raised serious questions. The Youth Justice Board (2006) looked at those issued to those aged under 18 in ten areas of England and Wales between January 2004 and January 2005. It found that:

■ There was wide geographical variation in the use of ASBOs.

■ 49 per cent of young people breached their ASBO at least once.

■ 22 per cent of young people given ASBOs were black or Asian – two and a half times the proportion of people from minority ethnic groups in England and Wales.

■ Many young people did not understand the restrictions placed upon them by their ASBO.

■ The overuse of ASBOs led many to regard them as a 'badge of honour'.

These findings, and the difficulties of defining what 'antisocial' means, reveal the unintended consequences of legislating against behaviour that might be widely considered troublesome but which depends on *perceptions*, but not necessarily *proof*, of harm (proof of harm is required in criminal cases). Geographical variation and apparent discrimination suggest little consistent understanding of what constitutes antisocial behaviour, how it might be identified and how it might best be responded to.

2.2 Juridification and criminalisation

In considering the definition of antisocial behaviour and its relationship to personal security, we have identified one key area in which welfare policies and crime control policies interact. Bringing civil law to bear upon social behaviour is new, but the tendency for more and more behaviour to be subject to legal regulation was already well established. The concept of *juridification* draws attention to the proliferation of law in regulating behaviour. Law is increasingly used in formulations and enforcements of 'acceptable behaviour' in the field of welfare. Juridification sees everyday social relations becoming increasingly circumscribed by criminal and civil law, and interpersonal conflicts being solved with reference to it (see Chapter 1, Section 4.4). However, juridification also implies that individuals increasingly see themselves as belonging to a community of legal subjects with equal legal rights. They will entrust the protection of their personal freedom to the legal system rather than to other allegiances and loyalties, private obligations or reciprocities.

These two facets of juridification capture an important tension. On the one hand, increased juridification represents a breakdown of the implied social contract through which such relations were managed within families, neighbourhoods and communities, and in this context the kinds of orders imposed on antisocial behaviour might be seen as a heavy-handed application of law to a range of largely imagined threats or behaviours that traditionally were dealt with in other ways. On the other hand, it defines society as a set of individuals and groups who have separate but equal interests that have to be asserted against each other. As such, orders imposed on antisocial behaviour may also be interpreted as a means of protecting a vulnerable majority (the public) from the threatening actions of a troubled minority.

This reframing of social relations makes it possible to see how *criminalisation* becomes a corollary of juridification. Criminalisation refers to the institutionalised process through which certain acts and behaviours are selected and labelled as 'crimes' and through which particular individuals and groups are subsequently selectively identified and differentially policed and disciplined. To the extent that ever more categories of conduct become subject to law, in so far as they contravene another group's rights (to security, for example), more actions become defined as illegal and more people become defined as 'criminal'. In the case of ASBOs, the offenders are not, technically, criminals, since antisocial behaviour is a civil offence. But antisocial behaviour can and does lead directly to criminal prosecution in certain circumstances. As a result, young people's apparent threat to the well-being of others leads to their criminalisation.

The interconnected processes of juridification and criminalisation represent the entanglement of welfare and crime control. While the continual expansion and reach of the law can be punitive from the perspective of some groups, it may also be protective for others. Juridification and criminalisation may be used to protect the rights of the disadvantaged in the face of threats to personal security by powerful groups. In the following section, we will look at the example of 'hate crime' legislation, ostensibly introduced to protect vulnerable social groups.

3   Punishing prejudice

Activity 4.4

Consider the three cases set out below and answer these questions:

- What distinctive features do they have in common?

- What was the impact of these features on the sentences given?

- How do the threats to security posed by the actions described differ from the threats posed by antisocial behaviour?

- How might juridification and criminalisation affect other people's security in these cases?

1   In 1998, James Byrd Jnr, a middle-aged African American, was attacked by a group of white supremacists in Jasper, Texas, chained to the back of a truck and dragged for three miles until he was decapitated. Federal authorities successfully applied hate crime charges against his three attackers, which made them eligible for the death penalty. Two were subsequently sentenced to death; the third was sentenced to life imprisonment.

2 In 1999, David Copeland, a self-professed racist and homophobic, was convicted of nail bomb attacks in Brixton, Brick Lane and Soho after he had deliberately targeted and killed members of London's gay, lesbian and minority ethnic communities. A plea of diminished responsibility was not accepted and he was convicted of murder and received six life sentences.

3 A long-running dispute in San Jose, California in the 1990s between homosexual and heterosexual neighbours over the spilling of grass cuttings on each other's lawns escalated into violence coupled with anti-gay abuse. The heterosexual neighbour was subsequently convicted, not of simple assault, but of a hate-motivated assault, which is a felony (a serious, imprisonable offence).

Comment

All three offences were directed against certain individuals primarily because they were assumed to be *representative* of some identifiable group. In each case, the sentence was much more severe than it might otherwise have been. Murder and assault are already criminal offences. In these cases, the process of juridification differentiated the attacks from common murder or assault, labelling them as distinctive new crimes. By making this distinction, the sentencing threshold was raised in each case. This was intended as an enhanced deterrent that might protect the security of other potential victims.

3.1 Defining hate crime

Certain criminal acts, if perpetrated because of hostility, bias, or negative attitudes towards a group to which the victim is perceived to belong, have become defined as hate crimes. The concept can encompass a wide range of behaviours, including racist crime, sex crime, homophobia, religious hatred and sectarianism, and can also link across to ethnic cleansing, terrorism and genocide. Legislating specifically against hate originates from, and is strongest in, the USA. Other countries, including the UK, have slowly followed this lead.

The term hate crime originated in the mid 1980s, through the lobbying of civil rights groups in the USA to include data on offences motivated by race, religion, sexual orientation and ethnicity in criminal statistics. The intention was to raise public awareness that crime motivated by prejudice and bigotry would not be tolerated (Levin, 2002). In 1992 the US Congress defined a hate crime as a crime in which 'the defendant's conduct was motivated by hatred, bias, or prejudice, based on the actual or perceived race, colour, religion, national origin, ethnicity, gender, sexual orientation or gender identity of another individual or group of individuals'. In 1994, the federal Violent Crime Control and Law Enforcement Act added disabilities to this list. The Hate Crimes Prevention Acts of 1999 and 2005 further strengthened the law by advocating a lower burden of proof to proceed with hate crime prosecutions. Many states have also developed their own legislation, but significantly not all include gender-based, sexual orientation-based or disability-based crimes.

Hate crime legislation in the UK is more recent and less broad. Incitement to racial hatred was first recognised as an offence in the Race Relations Act 1965. The Public Order Act 1986 subsequently criminalised the use of words or behaviour and possession of material considered 'threatening, abusive or insulting' and which was intended to, or likely to, stir up racial hatred. It is notable that this early legislation focused on 'incitement' rather than 'hate crime' itself: the term 'hate crime' has never specifically appeared in any UK legislation and only began to emerge in policy as a result of the official inquiry into the racist murder of Stephen Lawrence in 1993 (Bowling and Phillips, 2000). The Crime and Disorder Act 1998 moved closer to the American position by introducing 'racially aggravated offences'. This allowed for additional penalties to be applied to existing offences if motivated by racial hostility. The Anti-terrorism, Crime and Security Act 2001 extended this to religious hostility, apparently designed to help protect Muslim communities after the 9/11 attack on the World Trade Center. The Criminal Justice Act 2003, whilst not creating specific offences, also allowed for sentencing enhancement of offences motivated by homophobia and disability bias. The Racial and Religious Hatred Act 2006 created new offences of stirring up hatred on religious grounds, thereby targeting those whose offences are driven by hatred of the beliefs, or *lack* of such beliefs, of others.

3.2 Symbolic crimes, symbolic legislation?

Two examples demonstrate the complexity of hate crime, and the difficulties of including particular behaviours within the remit of criminal law.

The Jena Six

On 30 August 2006, in Jena, Louisiana, a black high school student sought permission to sit under a shady tree at break times, in an area usually used by white students. He was told he was free to sit where he wanted to. The next day nooses were found hanging from the tree. After some debate within the school, the three white pupils found responsible were given 'in-school suspensions' which required them to attend another school for a few days.

On 4 December 2006, in an ostensibly unrelated incident, although occurring amidst growing tensions, a white student from the school was assaulted, though not seriously hurt. Six black students (the 'Jena Six') were charged with conspiracy to commit second-degree murder. One, Mychal Bell (16 years old), was convicted on charges of aggravated second-degree battery and conspiracy to commit aggravated second-degree battery. He faced an extended prison term before the charges were reduced after a state appeals court ruled that he should not have been tried as an adult. At the end of 2007, a prison sentence remained a possibility, while the cases of the other five were still to be tried.

Undoubtedly, the nooses were a racially motivated threat that might easily be described as a hate crime, particularly because they recall the racist campaigns of the Ku Klux Klan, whose members lynched many thousands of black men and women in incidents like the decapitation of James Byrd Jnr described in Activity 4.4. Yet the white students' actions were dealt with as minor internal disciplinary matters and the police, a representative of the FBI, and the US Attorney's Office claimed initially that they did not meet the criteria for a federal hate crime. Only later, in October 2007, did federal prosecutor Donald Washington argue that the actions constituted a hate crime but the students were not so charged because they were juveniles (Fears, 2007).

Figure 4.3

Confrontation between black citizens and members of the Ku Klux Klan in Lakeland, Florida, August 1938

It is unclear whether there was any connection between the noose incident and the attack, or whether the attack was a premeditated or coordinated act. However, campaigners for the Jena Six have highlighted the differences in the treatment of the white and black students. Had the incident been interpreted as a hate crime from the start to punish the 'symbolic crime' of hanging nooses from the tree, the treatment of the two groups of students may have been perceived to be more equal. Should such 'symbolic crimes' be held as equivalent to crimes caused by physical violence, or might a prosecution that perceives them as equal also impact upon free speech and free expression, which is a constitutional right in the USA? This case demonstrates in many ways the difficulty in pursuing justice through the criminal law, in determining exactly what constitutes 'hate crime', and in determining whether incitement and physical violence should be given the same status. (For a more detailed timeline of events, see thejenatimes.net, 2008).

Holocaust denial

The genocide of the Holocaust during the Second World War (when six million Jews were killed) is an unambiguous example of a hate crime and few people dispute that it was a heinous one, motivated by racial hatred. But even here there are complexities. Is it a (hate) crime to deny that a hate crime took place, despite unequivocal evidence? In 2006, the UK historian David Irving was sentenced to three years' imprisonment for a speech he made in 1989 in which he claimed that there were no gas chambers at the Nazi concentration camp at Auschwitz. The speech was made in Austria, a country whose laws make it a criminal offence to deny the Holocaust. Nine other European countries, excluding the UK, have similar laws: had Irving made the speech in the UK he would not have committed a specified offence. Had he done so since the 1998 Crime and Disorder Act, it is unclear whether he would have been guilty of a 'racially aggravated offence', though it seems unlikely. Should Holocaust denial be classified as a hate crime, and be punishable as a criminal offence? What is the purpose of such legislation? The issue here is to consider what the implications of denying that history might be. It might be judged that denying the Holocaust provides a basis on which the (undeniably racist) politics that underpinned it might be legitimated once again.

In themselves, the Jena nooses were grossly provocative and profoundly threatening to all black students, but it was the absence of *direct* physical harm that was presented as the rationale for the lenient response (though this leaves out of account the subsequent harsh treatment of the six black students, which seems to exemplify the trends of mass imprisonment and black over-representation in US prisons described in Chapter 1, Section 4.1). Similarly, Irving's speech did no direct material harm to any individual, despite denigrating the suffering of millions and profoundly distressing their families. This too may explain Irving's release from jail on probation after just one year of his sentence. The 'crime', in both cases, is primarily *symbolic*, in that it *recalls* specific aspects of past racist atrocities. In the eyes of many commentators, the principal purpose of hate crime legislation is not to facilitate the prosecution of acts of bigotry. Rather, it is to match symbolic crimes with *symbolic legislation* – legislation that is intended as a clear assertion of dominant norms and values which might, in extreme cases, be pursued in law. This is *not* to suggest that all hate crime legislation is merely symbolic, still less that all hate crimes are symbolic. The examples of the Ku Klux Klan and the Nazis are emblems of history's most appalling atrocities. Nonetheless, the legislation *is* intended as a deterrent as well as a means of punishing gross harms based on prejudice.

3.3 Universal and minority rights

Hate crime legislation has been consistently controversial. A central issue is whether protection against victimisation is best served by the criminal law or human rights legislation. Hate crime law is usually advocated as a strategy which promotes tolerance by safeguarding cultural diversity. But is this necessarily the case? Some critics maintain that the criminal law is not appropriate for adjudicating on issues of what amount to 'identity politics' (Jacobs and Potter, 1998). Responses to intolerance ultimately need to move beyond legislation to address the economic and cultural conditions in which prejudice, resentment and hatred escalate. Similarly, we can ask whether judicial impartiality and legal 'due process' can be met when laws are designed to punish twice: once for the act itself and a second time for the speech or thought that motivated it. The process of legislating and/or enhancing sentencing in these areas has indeed been critiqued from all sides of the political spectrum, and on a number of grounds:

- The criminalisation of attitude, speech and thought feeds into populist demands for ever-tougher punishments to deal with crime and social problems.

- Civil rights/affirmative action agendas politicise the crime problem and corrupt the core principles of criminal law, due process and rules of evidence.

- The criminalisation of hate legitimises initiatives to stamp down on any form of 'undesirable' racially and religiously motivated behaviour, leading to censorship.

- In the wake of 9/11 attacks on the twin towers of New York's World Trade Center and the ensuing 'war on terror', hate legislation may facilitate greater suspicion of minority interests, not tolerance and protection as intended. It may legitimate increases in controls on immigration and asylum in the name of protecting an 'inclusive sense of citizenship'.

■ The fragmentation of criminal law into various offender and victim positions heightens tensions and *reinforces* prejudices and mutual suspicions.

■ Definitional difficulties have resulted in the creation of laws that are too broad in scope and too vague to enforce. Their impact is, as you have seen, more *symbolic* than a viable means of punishing offenders or preventing hate (Hall, 2005).

In contrast, other writers such as Jenness and Broad (1997) have argued that it is only through the adoption of such legislation that the nature, extent and atrocities of hate can be publicly recognised and acted against. Perry (2001) lays claim to the potential of law in asserting the legitimacy of minority group identities and in the shaping and valuing of a 'positive politics of difference'. Similarly, McLaughlin (2002) has argued that identifying and legislating against hate should be viewed as integral to articulating the values of safe multicultural societies, including public recognition, and affirmation, of the 'right to be different'.

Figure 4.4

Members of the Westboro Baptist Church in Kansas, USA claim that 'tolerance of homosexuality' is responsible for the deaths of victims of AIDS, war, terrorism and disaster. Their death is 'God's revenge'. In 2007, the church was fined $10.9 million for picketing the funeral of a soldier killed in Iraq, but their actions have not been officially designated as a 'hate crime'

These debates are particularly complex and vexed. The specific intention to criminalise and punish 'hate' takes the criminal justice system into an uncharted territory of adjudicating certain kinds of thought and speech whose seriousness is difficult to establish objectively. The concept of 'hate crime' conjures up images of a highly emotive crime committed by extremists, but research in the UK (Ray et al., 2004) and the USA (Jacobs and Potter, 1998) concludes that the majority of reported hate crimes relate to 'low-level' graffiti and harassment in which 'hate language' is employed, but typically by children, not serious offenders.

The irrational hatred of anonymous strangers who become objects of anger and violence by virtue of their identities, not their personal conduct, poses a particular set of challenges to enhancing security in times of perceived dangerousness. Undoubtedly fuelled by threats of terror visited by one culture or nation upon another, undiscriminating hostility towards anonymous others might at first sight appear a rational defence of security against perceived aggressors. But the logic of hating people by virtue of their identities generalises easily into mutual hatreds. Making a special case for hate crime by lowering the thresholds of proof for conviction or applying the severest penalties is therefore, in the view of its advocates, essential for minimising personal feelings of insecurity and establishing the conditions of an inclusive multicultural citizenship.

As with antisocial behaviour, then, it is the security and welfare of victims of *generalised* hatred that is at the heart of identifying the offence of hate crime. Whether it is perpetrated by individuals acting independently, whether it is motivated by racism or homophobia (as in the examples in Activity 4.4), whether it is politically motivated as a collective expression of racial hatred (as in the Holocaust), or whether it is a much more symbolically defined racially aggravated offence (as in Jena), the identification of hate crime constitutes a juridificatory extension of the reach of law and an extension of the power of the state designed to promote the welfare of some groups at the expense of the 'liberty' of others.

4 Measuring hate and incivility: quantitative data as evidence

You have seen the difficulties of defining certain acts based on prejudice and incivility. Should we then expect that the extent of such behaviours is capable of being measured reliably? Statistical evidence is routinely used to assess the nature and extent of certain behaviours. A key element involves 'gathering' data on risks, probabilities, recorded occurrences, trends, and so on. So, according to the Home Office (2005), there were 35,022 racially or religiously aggravated offences recorded by the police in England and Wales in 2003/04. Of these, 59 per cent were harassment, 16 per cent criminal damage, 14 per cent other wounding, and 11 per cent common assault. However, police forces varied widely in the number and type of offences recorded.

The common justification for collecting such data is that without having faith in the 'facts', and unless outcomes are measured in a reliable, consistent and valid fashion, governments cannot 'know' if their policies are working. Surely, it is argued, statistical evidence is more dependable than presupposition, hearsay or 'blind faith'? Indeed, 'counting' has a central place in government policymaking. It is premised on the idea that properly formulated 'scientific' research can not only reveal the extent of social problems, but also 'what works' for their resolution.

Activity 4.5

Government statistics are frequently presented as authoritative. They are routinely turned to by policymakers and academics. Already in this chapter statistics have been used to illustrate the association of young people with antisocial behaviour, as well as in noting increases in racially and religiously aggravated offences. But how reliable is this data and how much faith should we place in it? This activity is designed to start you thinking critically about the process whereby official, and, in particular, criminal, statistics are constructed by looking at statistics on hate and incivility.

Examine the statistics on antisocial behaviour, in Table 4.2, produced by the Home Office; the data on 'racist hate crime', in Table 4.3, collected by the Scottish Executive; and the 'bias motivations', in Table 4.4, recorded by the US Department of Justice, and make notes on the trends, local differences and causes of bias they seem to indicate.

Table 4.2 Number of Anti-social Behaviour Orders issued at all courts in England and Wales, as reported to the Home Office by the Court Service by area and year, April 1999 to December 2005

CJS Area	Total issued	Apr 99 - May 00 Total	Jun 00 - Dec 00 Total	2001 Total	2002 Total	2003 Total	2004 Jan-Mar	Apr-Jun	Jul-Sep	Oct-Dec	Total	2005 Jan-Mar	Apr-Jun	Jul-Sep	Oct-Dec	Total
Avon & Somerset	222	9	3	19	10	31	16	20	32	21	89	27	12	11	11	61
Bedfordshire	82	0	0	4	4	16	1	4	9	4	18	5	19	6	10	40
Cambridgeshire	101	5	1	2	2	15	8	6	9	3	26	14	15	11	10	50
Cheshire	208	0	0	2	13	33	8	20	14	20	62	27	30	29	12	98
Cleveland	116	1	4	4	5	14	4	3	7	14	28	15	13	17	15	60
Cumbria	116	1	1	1	13	20	4	8	9	10	31	11	15	14	9	49
Derbyshire	128	3	7	6	2	10	9	17	12	8	46	16	13	11	14	54
Devon & Cornwall	178	1	0	10	3	12	3	22	31	24	80	30	16	18	8	72
Dorset	77	0	2	3	0	17	6	6	18	6	36	3	6	6	4	19
Durham	96	0	5	9	8	16	9	8	4	10	31	4	10	6	7	27
Essex	149	0	0	0	2	16	11	9	15	24	59	26	25	15	6	72
Gloucestershire	68	0	2	2	1	7	3	5	8	10	26	14	12	3	1	30
Greater London	1172	9	19	15	21	139	84	94	133	130	441	154	143	118	113	528
Greater Manchester	1237	10	2	25	78	236	101	100	114	115	430	124	133	115	84	456
Hampshire	273	1	2	6	10	43	17	27	28	27	99	32	34	27	19	112
Hertfordshire	146	1	1	9	6	17	13	11	12	4	40	21	17	20	14	72
Humberside	236	0	9	4	4	10	4	14	27	27	72	36	36	36	29	137
Kent	159	0	3	17	16	25	6	19	11	18	54	14	12	10	8	44
Lancashire	362	5	5	11	13	54	27	25	38	36	126	33	38	44	33	148
Leicestershire	121	1	4	0	1	15	6	4	10	21	41	28	16	4	11	59
Lincolnshire	43	0	0	2	2	7	5	1	4	2	12	5	5	5	5	20
Merseyside	308	8	3	7	22	44	24	20	25	27	96	39	41	21	27	128
Norfolk	123	6	0	12	9	7	7	8	17	11	43	13	13	12	8	46
Northamptonshire	85	1	2	5	1	6	3	12	8	16	39	13	8	9	1	31
Northumbria	309	7	5	9	16	25	10	16	16	32	74	51	53	42	27	173
North Yorkshire	95	4	0	7	0	9	8	9	11	13	41	10	3	11	10	34
Nottinghamshire	256	1	4	11	2	21	14	18	22	37	91	41	28	34	23	126
South Yorkshire	248	3	1	7	19	34	9	20	25	26	80	34	25	17	28	104
Staffordshire	170	0	4	6	12	30	13	8	25	13	59	14	21	16	8	59
Suffolk	168	3	0	4	5	25	11	16	25	26	78	11	18	10	14	53
Surrey	110	0	2	2	2	7	7	13	13	15	48	14	13	12	10	49
Sussex	248	3	4	3	16	31	6	34	25	32	97	22	29	22	21	94
Thames Valley	163	1	1	7	6	16	12	18	31	16	77	16	12	12	15	55
Warwickshire	87	0	1	2	15	11	9	5	6	8	28	6	9	11	4	30
West Mercia	236	5	8	39	30	28	8	13	15	20	56	10	24	18	18	70
West Midlands	787	11	28	58	30	119	36	51	63	88	238	92	81	83	47	303
West Yorkshire	696	4	2	14	14	97	86	80	69	70	305	58	61	65	76	260
Wiltshire	52	0	0	0	1	9	6	6	4	4	20	7	8	5	2	22
England	9431	104	135	344	414	1272	614	770	945	988	3317	1090	1067	926	762	3845
Dyfed Powys	35	0	0	0	0	12	4	2	2	0	8	1	2	5	7	15
Gwent	72	0	0	2	2	8	4	5	9	9	27	7	14	7	5	33
North Wales	168	0	1	0	7	15	9	6	12	15	42	23	31	29	20	103
South Wales	147	0	1	4	3	29	4	12	18	12	46	15	15	18	16	64
Wales	422	0	2	6	12	64	21	25	41	36	123	46	62	59	48	215
Total E&W	9853	104	137	350	426	1336	635	795	986	1024	3440	1136	1129	985	810	4060

Note 1: Previously issued data have been revised following joint Home Office/Court Service data reconciliation exercises.

Note 2: Every effort is made to ensure that the figures presented are accurate and complete. However, it is important to note that these data have been extracted from large administrative data systems generated by the courts. As a consequence, care should be taken to ensure data collection processes and their inevitable limitations are taken into account when those data are used.

Source: Home Office, 2006, Table A2

Table 4.3 Racist incidents recorded by the police in Scotland, by local authority area, 2003/04 to 2005/06

Local Authority	2003/04[1]		2004/05		2005/06	
	Number	Rate per 10,000 Population	Number	Rate per 10,000 Population	Number	Rate per 10,000 Population
Aberdeen City	231	11.2	314	15.4	267	13.2
Aberdeenshire	51	2.2	86	3.7	75	3.2
Angus	38	3.5	46	4.2	66	6.0
Argyll & Bute	25	2.7	33	3.6	25	2.8
Clackmannanshire			51	10.6	51	10.5
Dumfries & Galloway	53	3.6	78	5.3	89	6.0
Dundee City	192	13.4	217	15.3	246	17.3
East Ayrshire	65	5.4	75	6.3	67	5.6
East Dunbartonshire	41	3.8	41	3.8	33	3.1
East Lothian	29	3.2	28	3.1	38	4.1
East Renfrewshire	43	4.8	48	5.4	55	6.1
Edinburgh, City of	519	11.6	607	13.4	976	21.3
Eilean Siar	7	2.7	18	6.9	12	4.6
Falkirk			162	11.0	182	12.2
Fife	343	9.7	302	8.5	241	6.8
Glasgow City	1,066	18.5	1,226	21.2	1,277	22.1
Highland	100	4.8	97	4.6	107	5.0
Inverclyde	48	5.8	32	3.9	36	4.4
Midlothian	31	3.9	52	6.5	82	10.4
Moray	30	3.4	38	4.3	44	5.0
North Ayrshire	67	4.9	91	6.7	103	7.6
North Lanarkshire	180	5.6	181	5.6	207	6.4
Orkney Islands	0	0.0	4	2.1	4	2.0
Perth & Kinross	60	4.4	70	5.1	93	6.7
Renfrewshire	101	5.9	131	7.7	86	5.1
Scottish Borders	33	3.0	26	2.4	43	3.9
Shetland Islands	9	4.1	4	1.8	5	2.3
South Ayrshire	40	3.6	42	3.8	64	5.7
South Lanarkshire	98	3.2	162	5.3	181	5.9
Stirling			73	8.5	129	14.8
West Dunbartonshire	62	6.7	90	9.8	82	9.0
West Lothian	81	5.0	111	6.8	158	9.6
Scotland	3,643	7.2	4,536	8.9	5,124	10.1

[1] Central Scotland police force were unable to supply data for 2003/04.

Source: Scottish Executive, 2007, p. 11, Table 2

Table 4.4 USA: incidents, offences, victims and known offenders by bias motivation, 2004

Bias motivation	Incidents	Offenses	Victims[1]	Known offenders[2]
Total	7,649	9,035	9,528	7,145
Single-Bias Incidents	7,642	9,021	9,514	7,136
Race:	4,042	4,863	5,119	4,173
Anti-White	829	998	1,027	1,085
Anti-Black	2,731	3,281	3,475	2,694
Anti-American Indian/Alaskan Native	83	97	100	97
Anti-Asian/Pacific Islander	217	252	266	188
Anti-Multiple Races, Group	182	235	251	109
Religion:	1,374	1,480	1,586	604
Anti-Jewish	954	1,003	1,076	330
Anti-Catholic	57	57	68	37
Anti-Protestant	38	43	48	28
Anti-Islamic	156	193	201	124
Anti-Other Religion	128	140	147	68
Anti-Multiple Religions, Group	35	37	39	14
Anti-Atheism/Agnosticism/etc.	6	7	7	3
Sexual Orientation:	1,197	1,406	1,482	1,258
Anti-Male Homosexual	738	855	902	832
Anti-Female Homosexual	164	201	212	163
Anti-Homosexual	245	297	314	224
Anti-Heterosexual	33	35	36	22
Anti-Bisexual	17	18	18	17
Ethnicity/National Origin:	972	1,201	1,254	1,047
Anti-Hispanic	475	611	646	585
Anti-Other Ethnicity/National Origin	497	590	608	432
Disability:	57	71	73	54
Anti-Physical	23	23	24	16
Anti-Mental	34	48	49	38
Multiple-Bias Incidents[3]	7	14	14	9

[1] The term *victim* may refer to a person, business, institution, or society as a whole.

[2] The term *known offender* does not imply that the identity of the suspect is known, but only that an attribute of the suspect has been identified, which distinguishes him/her from an unknown offender.

[3] In a multiple-bias incident two conditions must be met: (1) more than one offence type must occur in the incident and (2) at least two offence types must be motivated by different biases.

Source: US Department of Justice, 2005, p. 9, Table 1

Figures collected for the Home Office show a dramatic rise in the issuing of ASBOs in England and Wales, from 104 in 1999/00 to 4060 in 2005/06, with Greater Manchester and Greater London being the most 'antisocial' places. The statistics on racist incidents in Scotland appear to reveal a growing trend from 3643 in 2003/04 to 5124 in 2005/06, with Glasgow the most 'racist' local authority area. The statistics for the USA from 2004 appear to show a 'bias motivation' operating most strongly in terms of race (anti-black), religion (anti-Jewish), and sexual orientation (anti-male homosexuality).

How should we interpret such figures? Do they necessarily show that the problems of race hatred and incivility are becoming steadily worse? Or do they prove that government policy has been successful in 'tracking down' undesirable behaviours and making them publicly visible? Increases in crime rates can indeed suggest both *failure* and *success* in the fight against crime.

How else might these statistics be explained? Think, first, of the impact of new legislation; second, of the (perhaps) higher propensity of the public to report such offences due to greater political/media visibility; and, third, of a greater willingness on the part of the police to use these categories to record offences.

Comment

As the Scottish Executive report (in which Table 4.3 appeared) pointed out, these figures should indeed be received with some caution because they referred only to instances recorded by the police and therefore quite probably did not include all racist incidents. Moreover, because of the implementation (from April 2004) of the Scottish Crime Recording Standard, corroborative evidence was no longer required initially to record a crime-related incident as a crime as long as it was perceived as such by the victim. Much of the rise in racial incidents since then may thus be due solely to changes in public reporting and police recording practices. Similarly, the footnote to the statistical table on antisocial behaviour in England and Wales stresses that the 'inevitable limitations' of the data should be taken into account. Equally the identification of 'known offenders' in the data for the USA appears reliant on victims' perceptions of various offender 'attributes' which again are likely to be subjective.

In general, statistical data should be approached with caution. First, statistics on 'crime' depend on which harms, troubles and conflicts are defined as worthy of a legal response and which are not. Second, they cannot hope to be a reflection of actual crime rates because they are indices only of those crimes that are reported to and taken seriously by the police. For example, the *British Crime Survey* (based on reports from victims, rather than police records) estimates that only 50 per cent of offences are reported to the police, and of these 40 per cent are not recorded. This suggests a difference of 70 percentage points between victim experience and official statistics (assuming that victims themselves are telling the truth!).

Changes in offence classification can also lead to dramatic, but entirely unwarranted, 'revelations' about crime waves and crime seriousness. For example, in 2000 official statistics suggested there had been an overall fall in the crime rate, but an increase in violent offences. The political and media response focused characteristically on the second of these 'conclusions'. Much of this apparent rise in violence has however subsequently been explained by the creation in 1998 of a new offence of 'common assault' which was introduced to discourage the police practice of disregarding or 'cuffing' minor offences (i.e. 'hiding' them up the police officer's cuff). We can similarly query the ever-upwards trend of antisocial behaviour and racial incidents during the decade 1997–2006, because of increases in legislation and the peculiarities of offence classification.

The more intolerant a society is of violence, it appears, the more violent crime will be recorded. The less secure a society perceives itself to be, the more measures of security are advocated. This is a vicious circle with a clear self-perpetuating outcome. Research evidence which suggests a more positive picture of the extent of crime and its seriousness is typically drowned out in a climate where public anxieties are constantly regenerated – especially those surrounding 'unruly youth' and the 'unassimilated immigrant'.

When faced with the question of whether these behaviours (and crime in general) are becoming more (or less) prevalent, the most apposite answer may be to accept that we do not truly know. Nevertheless, the statistics are not meaningless. They do tell us something about the social, legal and organisational priorities and constraints of the criminal justice system. Moreover, quantitative data continues to be routinely relied upon (albeit selectively) to justify particular acts of policymaking.

The key questions we should ask of all quantitative data are:

- Is it only numbers and numerical values that can 'count' as evidence?

- For what purpose were these statistics compiled, by whom, and with what effects on how they have been selected and presented?

- Are social meanings and interactions amenable to quantitative measurement?

- Are all aspects of the 'real world' knowable through statistics?

5 Thinking critically about juridification and criminalisation

So far, the emergence of antisocial behaviour and hate crime legislation has been used to illustrate different ways of thinking about the relationships between welfare, policies of crime control and security. Antisocial behaviour policies address perceived threats to people's security by extending the reach of civil law into social conduct. Hate crime legislation is claimed to protect vulnerable groups against tangible assaults on their security by lowering the threshold of proof and/or enhancing the deterrent power of sentences. Both, however, mark a significant extension of the law – what we have described as juridification – into what constitutes 'acceptable' behaviour. In this section we explore how crime control is also being decentralised, taken out of the hands of the state and made a key obligation for communities and families. We also consider whether it is possible to pursue welfare and security *without* recourse to formal criminal law, by looking at the example of restorative justice.

5.1 Decentralisation: 'governing at a distance'

Growing concern with security is fundamental to changes in the relationship between welfare and the control of crime. For example, concern with the welfare of victims of hostile conduct tends to be foregrounded at the expense of that of offenders. But some forms of welfare provision can also incorporate corrective (if not overtly punitive) strands. In Chapter 1, Section 4.3, you saw how Rose's (1999) theory of *responsibilisation* argued that programmes of activity like welfare-to-work are essential parts of the process of drawing in 'excluded' young people. Chapter 1, Section 4 also noted Garland's (2001) identification of a shift to policies of *preventative partnership* designed not to punish but to induce and reward approved forms of behaviour so that they replace punishable behaviours. Some civil 'orders' – making good damage, community service – are of this nature. Here the worlds of the promotion of welfare through crime prevention and the potential punishment of those who decline to participate in welfare programmes meet. People whose behaviour is deemed antisocial are the object of interventions designed to change their behaviour, in ways that might be labelled 'welfare', while those who refuse certain welfare interventions (directly or on behalf of their children) are seen as open to prosecution. Parents whose children are persistent truants (in the UK), for example, or people who refuse low-waged welfare-to-work jobs (in parts of the USA) are regarded as being 'at risk' and may be the subject of compulsion or even prosecution.

Garland's concept of *punitive segregation*, introduced in Chapter 1, Section 4, highlights a crucial shift from welfare and rehabilitation to the exclusion of those who are perceived as threats to security. Garland argues that the unsettling erosion of state-provided 'social security' is associated with enhanced fear of crime and demands for tougher penalties. The proliferation of perceptions of antisocial behaviour is seen alongside a loss of popular confidence in the state as *the* source of security. Self-protection is then seen as a rational response to perceived insecurities, and antisocial behaviour becomes identified as pre-criminal conduct best 'nipped in the bud'. Rose's theories identified strategies of control aimed at 'failed citizens' who must be reintegrated through locally developed programmes of activity, to steer them away from (re-)offending.

To Garland and to Rose, a more hierarchical and relatively centralised state is seen as having given way to *dispersed*, decentralised forms of governing, in which communities become self-managing and governments 'govern at a distance' through them. This implies less, rather than more, formal juridification. As a result, it becomes more difficult to say where the power to govern social problems like hate crime and antisocial behaviour is actually located. Theories of governmentality (see **Clarke, 2008**) try to explain how social order and socially approved conducts can be promoted by extending the 'reach' of governments' powers. As more and more agencies of welfare and crime control are empowered to reach into the everyday lives of targeted groups, so the powers of government are extended to manage how people conduct themselves. But at the same time governments' powers are also diluted by handing them over to more and more officials and professionals in welfare and criminal justice agencies, whose actions and decisions governments cannot monitor and control. These dilemmas and paradoxes are central to making sense of how communities are mobilised to manage (or fail to manage) people's behaviour (see **Mooney and Neal, 2009**; particularly **Hughes, 2009**).

5.2 Informality: restorative justice

The discussion of hate crime and antisocial behaviour has shown how conduct may become subject to legal sanction, how more people are drawn into formal systems of criminal justice as offenders, and how processes of state welfare can become extensions of the agencies of criminal justice. The juridification of both antisocial behaviour and hate crime entails criminalisation in the interests of personal security and welfare: in very different ways, the welfare of prospective victims is understood to be the driving consideration. Whatever the adverse effects of the juridification of hate and the criminalisation of the antisocial, the protection of vulnerable people means that these developments need to be understood in part as a radical reworking of a general welfare ethos.

However, there are important instances of a rather different trend, whereby welfare considerations have increasingly come to influence processes of criminal justice. As you saw in Chapter 1, Garland's (2001) analysis charts a shift away from a 'penal welfare complex' towards more punitive 'cultures of control'. But alongside this trend there have also emerged policies that are designed to facilitate *conflict resolution* in ways that not only take account of harms done to victims but also recognise the needs of offenders – and, more significantly, recognise the costs and the damage of excessively punitive responses to conflict. In other words, instead of a process of juridification or criminalisation, it might be argued that this is a process which removes issues from the criminal process, seeking to return them to forms of social negotiation.

In its purest version, the thinking of those who wish to reassert the welfare potential of intervention radically queries the state's right to take control of the resolution of conflicts. The Norwegian criminologist Nils Christie (1977) argues that conflicts (defined as 'crimes' by the state) have been 'stolen' from offenders and victims, who are their rightful 'owners', by the apparatus of criminal justice. This view maintains that orthodox thinking about crime, criminality and crime control is fundamentally flawed because the harms associated with social life cannot, and should not, be regulated by criminal justice systems. Conflicts, harms and antagonisms are an inevitable part of everyday life and their ownership is lost if they are delegated to professionals and legal specialists promising to provide 'expert solutions'. On this view, the formal criminal justice system does not achieve public protection, rehabilitation, deterrence or prevention. Rather, it causes unnecessary suffering and offers little benefit to victims or perpetrators. Juridification, criminalisation and resort to criminal law are seen as antithetical to 'achieving security'.

Such a radical critique turns instead to forms of justice that are built on entirely different principles from those operating in capitalist and other 'advanced' societies. Other bodies of law and long-standing cultural traditions upon which they are built have taken quite different approaches. In particular, the processes and cultural norms of a number of traditional indigenous societies have made fundamentally different responses to harms and conflicts. What these approaches have in common is that the perpetrator's legitimacy as a member of that community is paramount. Whatever action follows in response to harm to person or property must maintain and embed the offender's membership and standing, while also acknowledging the loss or hurt suffered by the victim. In particular, the response to the offence must view it as a conflict between the parties which the ensuing process must seek to resolve. Only by these means can social harmony and security be attained.

The generic term for this approach is 'restorative justice'. Justice is done by *restoring* well-being to the victim by some form of recognition or recompense, while the offender is *restored* to membership of the community by acknowledging the transgression. The term also refers to the restoration of the community to harmony, and to the restoration of the self-respect of victims and offenders. These restorations may take many forms: an apology, a demonstration of full recognition of the harm done, some repair of damage done to the individual or community, or acceptance of some form of shaming designed to strengthen communitarian ideals. The process may be ritual or ceremonial, it may involve release from restrictions, a public statement of forgiveness from the victim or community leaders, mentorship and guidance from a peer or elder, and so on. But central to all of these processes is the involvement of all those directly affected in the community, not just offender and victim. An anonymous, bureaucratic state has no role here: the conflict belongs to the community and must be resolved by it.

Aspects of this ideal-typical rendition of restorative justice can now be found in numerous jurisdictions. Here let's consider just three examples:

1   The employment of restorative principles to resolve conflict originates amongst the Maori of New Zealand, Australian Aboriginals, and the First Nation indigenous peoples of Canada and the USA. The procedures involved variously feature victim–offender mediation, community conferences, family group conferences, community sentencing circles, reparation agreements, and re-integrative shaming. The origins, precise form, conduct and effects of these procedures are, however, much debated. So is the efficacy of their adoption (and adaptation) in contemporary North America and Australasia, which continue to rely heavily on forms of retributive justice.

2   Arguably the most influential contemporary example of 'restoration' replacing 'retribution' as the guiding principle in achieving 'justice' is South Africa's Truth and Reconciliation Commission, following the abolition of apartheid (a state-sponsored hate crime?). The Commission was charged with investigating past human rights violations, granting amnesty for political crimes, and offering reparation to victims. Whatever the political expediency of this strategy (to counter the fear that formal prosecution of sections of the white population would only perpetuate violence), it was clear

that it involved a radical re-imagining of the nature of 'justice' and how it could be achieved. The notion that community relations could only be 'healed' through truth telling, forgiveness and acknowledgement of the harm done to past victims was clearly informed by restorative principles. It cemented the idea that lasting peace depended on establishing human rights provisions for long-term reconciliation. Subsequently, there have been misgivings about the precise meaning of 'reconciliation'. How far can individualised confession and forgiveness impact on a political context which readily witnesses the continuance of political and economic power in the hands of some former apartheid supporters? Does reconciliation simply mean an evasion of full accountability on the part of the powerful and an acceptance of structural inequalities on the part of the powerless?

3   In England and Wales, most of the policies inspired by restorative justice began to appear as small-scale local initiatives in youth justice in the 1990s, including restorative conferencing, restorative cautioning, and family conferencing. However, the Crime and Disorder Act 1998 and the Youth Justice and Criminal Evidence Act 1999 put restorative justice into the mainstream. Youth courts were provided with Referral Orders, through which they delegated disposals to Youth Offender Panels, which worked with offenders to establish contracts and programmes of activity, intended to increase a sense of responsibility. Victims were encouraged to participate in the panels. While there have been many positive comments about some aspects of the restorative benefits, there have been extensive reservations and criticisms, covering a range of concerns from high levels of local variation, incomplete implementation and drawing more people into the 'net' of being criminalised, to the coercion of participants, the continued predominance of professional over community power, very low levels of participation of victims and other community members, and, more generally, the re-bureaucratisation of what is intended to be an intensive process of interaction (Crawford and Newburn, 2003). The coexistence of ostensibly restorative measures alongside much more punitive approaches raises a more fundamental issue about the compatibility of restorative justice with otherwise retributive systems of justice (Daly, 2002).

The spread of restorative justice points to tensions and competing forces in the policies and purposes of systems of justice. It qualifies Garland's 'culture of control' thesis and reminds us that the resolution of conflict need not lie in a continual expansion of processes of juridification and criminalisation. Rather, a commitment to communitarian ideals, to community solidarity and to accountability might provide an important means of breaking out of the negative, vicious cycle of confrontation, hostility, resentment and retribution characteristic of formal criminal justice intervention (see, for example, Khan and Honeyman, 2007).

6 Review

This chapter has explored the proposition that much of what makes people feel secure can be traced to the ways in which policies concerning welfare and crime control interact. Growing preoccupation with incivilities and hatred appears not only to have triggered more legislation but also to have drawn numerous aspects of social and public policy – housing, race relations, youth work, family support, and many others – into a broader criminal justice agenda. The move to govern through communities (see **Mooney and Neal, 2009**) has also had the effect of bringing together a range of social and public policy agencies around disorder and crime. In some respects such developments can be viewed positively, particularly if their aim is to tackle the roots of conflict and dispute as much through social as through criminal justice intervention.

As you have seen, however, there are limits to this analysis, particularly when social policy and welfare do not drive, but are subjugated to, the goals of criminal justice. Early interventions actively seek out 'antisocial risk conditions' and behaviours ripe for prevention. Intervening to 'nip crime in the bud' also intensifies the processes of scrutiny and surveillance to which children and families are subjected. Legislating against antisocial and hate-driven behaviour may be primarily legitimated in the name of public protection, family support and community empowerment, but it also raises the prospect that 'social deficiencies are being redefined as "crime problems" which need to be controlled and managed rather than addressed in themselves' (Crawford, 1997, p. 230). Targeting 'risky' populations may exacerbate negative perceptions of particular localities or groups and accelerate their criminalisation. Legislating against hate may seriously backfire so that anyone can deny others whose opinions might be considered 'suspicious', 'subversive' or 'threatening'. Definitional ambiguities about what exactly constitutes hate and incivility may reinforce discriminatory interpretations of the behaviour of 'others'. Ambiguous or unreliable statistics and other evidence about the extent and nature of incivility and hatred exacerbate these problems, especially if they are exaggerated or misrepresented. The outcome of juridification in these areas may be more, rather than less, public fear and insecurity.

Finally, you have seen that many Western societies are experimenting with informal means of conflict resolution, especially restorative justice. Other bodies of law – economic, administrative, environmental, health, labour – rather than criminal law can be (and are being) drawn on to resolve disputes. Reforming the apparatuses of the criminal justice system has the potential to eliminate the problems generated by the system, such as the fabrication of guilt, the stigmatising of prisoners, the marginalisation and exclusion of certain powerless groups, institutionalised discrimination, the dramatisation of conflicts by the mass media, and the reproduction and perpetuation of violence. From this perspective, the agencies of the criminal justice system actively promote the belief that crime remains 'out of control', fuelled by the difficulties of establishing clear evidence that have been noted in this chapter. Following this line of argument suggests that juridification and criminalisation may generate more insecurity rather than less. Reforming the expensive, ineffective aspects of criminal justice could revitalise the pursuit of justice by allowing other forms of conflict resolution – redress, restoration and community justice – to be imagined and properly resourced.

Further reading

This chapter has introduced you to three distinct, overlapping modes of regulating social relations. These are civil justice (as represented in this chapter by antisocial behaviour legislation), criminal justice (as represented here by enhanced sentencing for hate crimes), and restorative justice (as represented here by informal means of conflict resolution). For critical commentaries on each of these see Elizabeth Burney's *Making People Behave: Antisocial Behaviour, Politics and Policy*, on the politics of antisocial behaviour legislation (2005, Willan); *Hate Crimes: Criminal Law and Identity Politics*, on hate crime and identity politics, by James Jacobs and Kimberly Potter (1998, Oxford University Press); and Kathleen Daly's paper 'Restorative justice: the real story', on the fundamental incompatibility of restorative justice and criminal justice, published in 2002 in *Punishment and Society*, vol. 4, no. 1, pp. 55–79.

References

Bowling, B. and Phillips, C. (2000) *Racism, Crime and Justice*, London, Pearson.

Burney, E. (2005) *Making People Behave: Antisocial Behaviour, Politics and Policy*, Uffculme, Willan.

Christie, N. (1977) 'Conflicts as property', *The British Journal of Criminology*, vol. 17, no. 1, pp. 1–15.

Clarke, J. (2008) 'Looking for social justice: welfare states and beyond' in Newman, J. and Yeates, N. (eds) (2008) *Social Justice: Welfare, Crime and*

Society, **Maidenhead, Open University Press/Milton Keynes,
The Open University.**

Crawford, A. (1997) T*he Local Governance of Crime*, Oxford, Oxford University Press.

Crawford, A. and Newburn, T. (2003) *Youth Offending and Restorative Justice*, Uffculme, Willan.

Daly, K. (2002) 'Restorative justice: the real story', *Punishment and Society*, vol. 4, no. 1, pp. 55–79.

Fears, D. (2007) 'US attorney calls noose display "hate crime", explains lack of charges', *Washington Post*, 17 October [online], http://www.washingtonpost.com/wp-dyn/content/article/2007/10/16/AR2007101600200.html (Accessed 26 March 2008).

Garland, D. (2001) *The Culture of Control: Crime and Order in Contemporary Society*, Oxford, Oxford University Press.

Hall, N. (2005) *Hate Crime*, Uffculme, Willan.

Harradine, S., Kodz, J., Lemetti, F. and Jones, B. (2004) *Defining and Measuring Anti-social Behaviour*, Development and Practice Report 26, London, Home Office; also available online at http://www.homeoffice.gov.uk/rds/pdfs04/dpr26.pdf (Accessed 7 March 2008).

Home Office (1997) *No More Excuses: A New Approach to Tackling Youth Crime in England and Wales*, London, Home Office; also available online at http://www.homeoffice.gov.uk/documents/jou-no-more-excuses (Accessed 16 January 2008).

Home Office (2005) *Statistics on Race and the Criminal Justice System – 2004*, London, HMSO; also available online at http://www.homeoffice.gov.uk/rds/pdfs05/s95race04.pdf (Accessed 8 March 2008).

Home Office (2006) 'Anti-social Behaviour Orders: statistics', Table A2 [online], http://www.crimereduction.homeoffice.gov.uk/asbos/asbos2.htm (Accessed 16 January 2008).

**Hughes, G. (2009) 'Community safety and the governance of "problem"
populations' in Mooney, G. and Neal, S. (eds)** *Community: Welfare, Crime and
Society*, **Maidenhead, Open University Press/Milton Keynes, The Open University.**

Jacobs, J. and Potter, K. (1998) *Hate Crimes: Criminal Law and Identity Politics*, Oxford, Oxford University Press.

Jenness, V. and Broad, K. (1997) *Hate Crimes: New Social Movements and the Politics of Violence*, New York, NY, Aldine.

Khan, B. and Honeyman, R. (2007) 'Restorative justice: a possible holistic response to combat hate crime', *Resolution 25*, London, Restorative Justice Consortium.

Labour Party (1995) *A Quiet Life: Tough Action on Criminal Neighbours*, London, Labour Party.

Levin, B. (2002) 'From slavery to hate crime laws: the emergence of race and status based protection in American criminal law', *Journal of Social Issues*, vol. 58, no. 2, pp. 227–45.

McLaughlin, E. (2002) 'Rocks and hard places: the politics of hate crime', *Theoretical Criminology*, vol. 6, no. 4, pp. 493–8.

Mooney, G. and Neal, S. (eds) (2009) *Community: Welfare, Crime and Society*, Maidenhead, Open University Press/Milton Keynes, The Open University.

Muncie, J. (2004) *Youth and Crime*, London, Sage.

Perry, B. (2001) *In the Name of Hate: Understanding Hate Crimes*, London, Routledge.

Ray, L., Smith, D. and Wastell, L. (2004) 'Shame, rage and racist violence', *British Journal of Criminology*, vol. 44, no. 3, pp. 350–68.

Rose, N. (1999) *Powers of Freedom: Reframing Political Thought*, Cambridge, Cambridge University Press.

Scottish Executive (2007) 'Racist incidents recorded by the police in Scotland, 2003/04 to 2005/06', *Statistical Bulletin*, March, Edinburgh, Scottish Executive; also available online at http://www.scotland.gov.uk/publications/2007/03/26094831/0 (Accessed 16 January 2008).

Squires, P. (2006) 'New Labour and the politics of antisocial behaviour', *Critical Social Policy*, vol. 26, no. 1, pp. 144–68.

10 Downing Street (2006) 'Morning press briefing from 10 January 2006' [online], http://www.number10.gov.uk/output/Page8901.asp (Accessed 8 March 2008).

thejenatimes.net (2008) 'Chronological order of events concerning the "Jena Six"' [online], http://www.thejenatimes.net/ChronologicalEvents.pdf (Accessed 26 March 2008).

US Department of Justice (2005) *Hate Crime Statistics, 2004*, Washington, DC, Federal Bureau of Investigation, US Department of Justice; also available online at http://www.fbi.gov/ucr/hc2004/tables/HateCrime2004.pdf (Accessed 16 January 2008).

Youth Justice Board (2006) *Antisocial Behaviour Orders*, London, YJB.

Chapter 5
War, disease and human security

Allan Cochrane and Deborah Talbot

Contents

1   Introduction

The uneasy tensions that lie at the heart of notions of 'security' have run through the chapters of this book. For a variety of reasons – the acceleration of social change and the attendant institutional, policy and legal transformations; the corrosion of welfare and job security; changes within the family; the growth of poverty, marginalisation and crime – the world seems a more insecure place. This insecurity is reinforced by a sense that our life experiences are increasingly shaped by events taking place apparently far away, yet also somehow close at hand. As **Cochrane and Walters (2008)** note, this is an interdependent world in which even apparently 'local' experiences involve sets of relationships which stretch much further afield (whether through patterns of consumption of food and cultural products, sources of income and investment, political and policy networks, or issues of environmental sustainability).

Activity 5.1

Look at the pictures in Figures 5.1 to 5.4. What issues do they raise about global interconnectedness and risk?

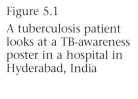
Figure 5.1
A tuberculosis patient looks at a TB-awareness poster in a hospital in Hyderabad, India

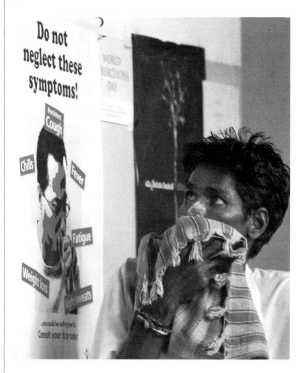

Figure 5.2
A warning sign near the Bernard Matthews poultry farm in Holton, Suffolk where there was an outbreak of bird flu in 2007

Figure 5.3
Customers queuing outside a Northern Rock branch waiting to remove their money from the crisis-hit bank, 2007; An employee carrying a box leaves the Enron building, Houston, Texas, during the build-up to the Enron financial scandal and bankruptcy, 2001

Figure 5.4
Afghan policemen and civilians carrying the body of the victim of a suicide car bombing in Kabul, 2006

Comment

In their different ways all these images suggest that patterns of risk are global. For example, resistant strains of tuberculosis (TB) have emerged in areas of the globe whose populations have lowered immune systems, and are transmitted through international travel. Avian flu has been transmitted by migrating wild birds and lax hygiene standards, affecting farms in Suffolk in 2007. The financial crisis which hit the British bank Northern Rock in 2007 was caused by its indirect involvement in the 'sub-prime' mortgage markets in the USA. A series of complex (and ultimately fraudulent) financial schemes attempting to take advantage of global markets in energy derivatives brought the Houston-based but internationally active Enron Corporation to bankruptcy in 2001. The war in Afghanistan which began in 2001 was originally launched by the USA and its allies in response to the attacks on New York's World Trade Center in that year. Afghanistan (then governed by the Taliban) was identified as a centre for global terrorism because it allowed Osama Bin Laden and other leaders of al-Qaeda to operate there. Some now argue that the likelihood of terror attacks in the UK has increased as a result of its involvement in Iraq and Afghanistan in the early part of the twenty-first century.

Many of our contemporary experiences reflect the increasing permeability of international interrelationships – breakthrough moments – where borders become potentially hazy. There is a growing perception both that similar risks may be widely shared and – more importantly – that risks emerging in one place may significantly affect the experience of those living elsewhere. This set of understandings has underpinned the development of forms of 'global' social policy, associated with international frameworks and institutions such as the United Nations, the World Trade Organization and the World Health Organization. It has also influenced thinking around the concept of 'human security', which we explore in this chapter.

The aims of this chapter are to:

- identify and explore some of the ways in which security is understood and managed at international or global level, in ways that directly affect everyday life (with a particular focus on the experience and consequences of war and disease)

- explore some of the institutional and regulatory arrangements that have emerged

- clarify some of the tensions embedded within human security, and explore the uneasy relationships between human security and national security

- draw critically on a wide range of evidence, with a particular concern for the ways in which evidence and public policy interact.

In preparation for these discussions, it is worth returning to some of the issues associated with the notion of human security referred to in Chapter 1. Since the end of the Second World War the maintenance of 'security' and the limitation of conflict between states have been central concerns of organisations such as the United Nations. In the mid 1990s, however, the concept of 'human security' was specifically introduced by the United Nations Development Programme (UNDP) as a means of reframing security as a 'human' issue rather than one solely concerned with national defence or military strategy. The argument was that, in the context of globalisation, international agendas needed to move away from a narrow focus on security, led by national defence and external and border threats, and focus instead on issues such as 'job security, income security, health security, environmental security, security from crime' (UNDP, 1994, p. 3). These issues were critical because, from the human security perspective, they undermined the prospects for development and, if not tackled, would lead to further social and global instability.

Activity 5.2

Disease and health are key policy areas for those concerned with human security. In 2003 the United Nations-sponsored Commission on Human Security, influenced by Amartya Sen (see Chapter 1, Section 2, Extract 1.2), set out some core principles which its authors believed were required to deliver human security in a global context. In the following extract we have included three of these principles. How might each of them interact with the spread of disease and ill health?

Extract 5.1

Protecting people in violent conflict

Civilians are the main casualties in conflicts. Both norms and mechanisms to protect civilians should be strengthened. This requires comprehensive and integrated strategies, linking political, military, humanitarian and development aspects. The Commission proposes placing human security formally on the agenda of security organizations at all levels. There are critical gaps in how human rights are upheld, in respect for citizenship and humanitarian law. These gaps need to be closed as well as attention given to ending the impunity of perpetrators of human rights violations. Community-based strategies to promote coexistence and trust among people will support these efforts. Equally urgent is meeting the life-saving needs of people through humanitarian assistance. Special attention should be given to protecting women, children, the elderly and other vulnerable groups. Disarming people and fighting crime through preventing the proliferation of weapons and illegal trade in resources and people has to be a priority.

...

Economic insecurity – the power to choose among opportunities

Extreme poverty remains pervasive. The proper functioning of markets as well as development of non market institutions are key to poverty eradication. Efficient and equitable trade arrangements, economic growth reaching the extreme poor and a fair distribution of benefits are essential. Together with addressing chronic poverty, human security focuses on sudden economic downturns, natural disasters and the social impacts of crises. To make people secure when crisis hits or to enable them to move out of poverty, we need social arrangements to meet their basic needs and ensure an economic and social minimum. Three-quarters of the world's people are not protected by social security or do not have secure work. Efforts to ensure sustainable livelihoods and work based security for all need to be strengthened. Access to land, credit, education, and housing, especially for poor women, is critical. An equitable distribution of resources is key to livelihood security and can enhance people's own capacity and ingenuity. Social protection measures and safety nets can advance a social and economic minimum. States, supported by the international system, need to establish early warning and prevention measures for natural disasters and economic or financial crises.

Health for human security

Despite the progress in healthcare, 22 million people died of preventable diseases in 2001. HIV/AIDS will soon become the greatest health catastrophe. In their urgency, depth and impact, global infectious diseases, poverty-related threats and health deprivations arising from violence are particularly significant. All health actors should promote health services as public goods. It is essential to mobilize social action and invest in supportive social arrangements, including the access to information, to remove the root causes of ill-health, to provide early warning systems and to mitigate health impacts once a crisis occurs. Providing access to life-saving drugs is critical for those in developing countries. An equitable intellectual property rights regime needs to be developed to balance incentives for research and development with ensuring people's access to affordable life-saving drugs. The international community must also form a global network of partnerships for health, promoting, for example, a global surveillance and control system for infectious diseases.

Commission on Human Security, 2003a

Comment

These three principles are merely part of a broader set of agendas around the protection and empowerment of populations situated in extreme situations. They do, however, illustrate how the human security framework focuses on the interdependent relationships between different social phenomena. War, inadequate health care, poverty and hunger all impact on the incidence and spread of disease. Likewise, the spread of infectious diseases and ill health themselves impact upon other sorts of indices of security, such as the ability to find or engage in employment.

Chen and Narasimhan (2003) argue that health and human security are linked in three ways: first, in the way that violence and war can precipitate health crises; second, through the threat of the spread of infectious diseases and toxins, whether the result of human behaviour or naturally occurring; third, in the way that poverty and inequality interact with human health and the delivery of health care. In the next two sections of this chapter, we look at two case studies which in their different ways enable us explore these three themes. In Section 2, we consider how civilians have been increasingly caught up in war and conflict, particularly through modern tactics of war focused on civilian infrastructure. In this section we explore how Iraq's water treatment facilities were caught up in war in the early 1990s, leading to the growth of infectious diseases. In Section 3, we consider the development of health policy and look at the case of HIV/AIDS, charting some of the ways in which disease and poverty interact. Throughout the chapter, we return to some of the core concepts of this book – punitivity, juridification, prevention, social protection and responsibilisation – and how they are expressed in the global (and conflicting) paradigms of national and human security, crime control and welfare.

2   Producing human insecurity: war and civilian infrastructures

It is undeniable, as the report of the Commission on Human Security notes (2003b), that we live in a world where war is normal for many and has had an increasing impact on civilian life. Since 1945 there have been 150 major wars with 23 million deaths resulting directly from them (Levy and Sidel, 1997a). These figures exclude more localised civil wars, and when they are taken into account the impact of violent conflict is still more striking. For example, between 1991 and 1994, 79 out of 82 wars were civil, and this included conflict in a third (16) of African states. The number is weighted towards recent history, with 34 conflicts occurring in 1994 alone (FitzSimons and Whiteside, 1994, p. 3). The public health impact of these conflicts ranges from malnutrition to a variety of diseases such as diphtheria, TB, hepatitis and dysentery caused by the displacing of populations, overcrowding, increases in prostitution, and the diversion of resources from health care to war.

Of course, civilians and civilian infrastructures have always been an object of war. But one key difference in the impact of wars in contemporary society is the scale of their impact on civilian life. Of the total killed in the First World War, for example, only 14 per cent were civilians. This increased to 67 per cent in the Second World War, 75 per cent in the 1980s, and 90 per cent in the 1990s (Garfield and Neugut, 1997, p. 33). One reason why civilians are more at risk of being casualties of war lies in their increasing concentration in cities. It has been estimated by the United Nations Population Fund (UNFPA) that in 2008 there will be 3.3 billion people living in towns and cities, over half of the world's population, with an estimated 4.9 billion by 2030. Most of this growth will take place in the developing world, and 'an outstanding feature of urban population growth in the twenty-first century is that it will be composed, to a large extent, of *poor* people' (UNFPA, 2007, p. 6). Urban overcrowding and the systems of dependencies created by cities have a peculiar poignancy in considering the impact of modern warfare on death and disease, particularly as it pertains to the poor.

2.1 War and urban infrastructure: a new military doctrine?

In the context of increasing urbanisation and the strategic importance of cities in recent years, new military tactics have been developed. In many ways we have been moving from the idea of war conducted through trained armies to one in which cities and civilians have become a key battleground of war. Central to this trend, argues Graham (2006), is the recasting of unstable spaces as dangerous places that breed rogue states or terror networks. The new tactics of war aim to 'secure' civilian life in the 'homeland' spaces of the West while those living in 'terrorist' spaces (such as Afghanistan) are themselves managed through new forms of military intervention.

Part of this approach to the conduct of war, directed against cities, is what Graham calls 'deliberate demodernisation', in which 'human security' itself becomes a military target of war. In other words, if your enemy has a fairly well-developed economy and infrastructure, weakening those core elements is one way of ensuring victory. However, such tactics are likely to produce high short-term and long-term civilian casualties, including women and children, who have traditionally been excluded from the mechanics of war. As King and Martin comment:

> [T]he 'bomb now, die later' implicit strategy of much present warfare (whereby a military campaign targets the public health infrastructure, from which many deaths occur after the bombing stops) is making war safer for soldiers and much riskier for civilians. The problem is not badly aimed guns, but rather the increasingly severe public health consequences of war.
>
> (King and Martin, 2001, p. 2)

Graham suggests that wars are not just fought *in* cities but *against* them. Strategies have been developed which have focused on the most effective way of weakening resistance through a doctrine known as 'effects-based operations' (Graham, 2005). According to this doctrine, the infrastructural assets of a country will be targeted simultaneously in order to instil chaos and therefore undermine military capability or resistance. For example, destroying a country's electrical supply and distribution systems will ultimately lead to a decreased capability by reducing the ability to: communicate and transport goods; access resources such as money; and have effective sanitation systems, cooking

Figure 5.5
Smoke billows from a building hit during an air raid in Baghdad in 2003

facilities, refrigeration, lighting, hospitals. All of this is in turn expected to lead to rising rates of disease, hunger and urban civilian decay, as well as severe problems in organising military strategy. One of these strategies – called the 'strategic ring theory' – was developed by US Air Force strategist John Warden in the USA and was used in the Iraq and Kosovan campaigns. It involved identifying systems of urban interdependency and using 'indirect' attacks on civilian infrastructures in order to pressurise and undermine political leadership (see Figure 5.6).

Although countries such as the USA argue that focusing on infrastructure leads to fewer direct civilian deaths and is therefore more humane, the impact of targeting infrastructure is more long-term in

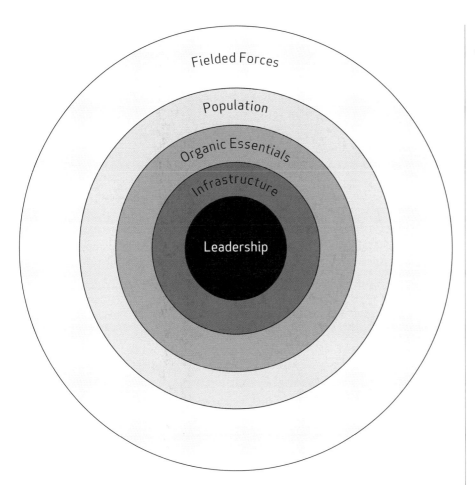

Figure 5.6
John Warden's 1995
'five-ring model' of the
strategic make-up of
contemporary societies
(Source: Graham, 2005,
p. 177, Figure 1)

that, as Graham argues, such emphases in contemporary warfare blur the distinction between wartime and peace, conflict and normalcy, by creating long-term consequences for human health. The case study in the following section considers one example where civilian infrastructure was targeted.

2.2 The war on Iraq, 1991, and water treatment facilities

In 1990 Iraq, whose president at the time was Saddam Hussain, invaded Kuwait. Despite Iraq being a key 'ally' of the USA during the Iran/Iraq war of 1980–88 and a recipient of aid, weapons and assistance with biological weapons research (see Reigle and D'Amato, 1994), the USA and other key allies, including the UK, imposed economic sanctions on Iraq followed by an invasion in 1991, termed Operation Desert Storm, commonly referred to as the First Gulf War. The war was notable for its unbalanced nature – Iraq having significantly less military capacity than the Allies – its speedy resolution, and for the targeting and destruction of 'dual use' facilities – electricity and other power supplies, telecommunications, ports, oil refineries, distribution networks, roads and bridges (Graham, 2005).

Before the 1991 war, Iraq was viewed as a rapidly industrialising nation, albeit not a democratic one. Fuelled by oil revenue, large investments had been made in civilian infrastructures such as health, education, food supply and sanitisation. Ninety-three per cent of Iraqis had access to safe water and health care (Care International/Johns Hopkins University, 2003, p. 4).

During the war, extensive bombing destroyed or incapacitated many aspects of civilian infrastructure, including bridges and roads, hospitals, communication centres, electrical supplies, water and sewerage facilities (Care International/Johns Hopkins University, 2003, p. 4). The latter has been perceived to be most devastating in terms of the impact on long-term public health. Iraq's water and sewerage systems were entirely reliant on electrical pumping stations. During the air strikes, 200 sorties were conducted against electrical plants, destroying or damaging 88 per cent of capacity. Over half of electrical generator sites in Iraq were totally destroyed. By the end of the war, the country was left with only 4 per cent of its pre-war capacity, with this rising to only 20–25 per cent four months later (Graham, 2005). There was little prospect for rebuilding the country's fairly sophisticated infrastructure after the war because of sanctions that prohibited any material that could be dual use – for use by the civilian or military sector – including water purification chemicals or any item required for repair. Macqueen et al. (2004, p. 111) argue that the extent of the problem was illustrated by estimates that by 1999 only 41 per cent of the population had access to safe drinking water, although such figures have been disputed, particularly for urban populations. It was noted in 2003, however, that 'the national output of potable water is presently only 40–60 per cent of pre-Gulf War levels' and, in 2000, 40 per cent of water samples were found to be contaminated (Care International/Johns Hopkins University, 2003, p. 11).

The lack of clean water has had a major impact on health. While only approximately 3000 civilians died in the air strikes in 1991, over 100,000 died of diseases such as gastro-enteritis, cholera and typhoid, diseases normally caused by lack of access to uncontaminated water (Macqueen et al., 2004). Typhoid increased from 113 per 100,000 of the population in 1990 to 142.1 per 100,000 of the population in 1994. Cholera increased from no reported cases in 1990 to 7.8 per 100,000 of the population in 1994. Other communicable diseases also increased, underpinned by a declining health service, specifically as a result of war and sanctions (Care International/Johns Hopkins University, 2003, pp. 17–18).

Activity 5.3

Thomas Nagy, Associate Professor of Expert Systems at George Washington University, played a major part in publicising a declassified document entitled 'Iraq water treatment vulnerabilities', produced by the USA Defence Intelligence Agency (DIA) in January 1991, the same month as the invasion. Extract 5.2 contains a series of excerpts from the document, one of a series of DIA documents predicting the impact of bombing and sanctions on the growth of disease. The document assesses the general strength of the water and sewerage systems in Iraq and outlines key vulnerabilities, particularly in the context of sanctions. In what ways could this policy analysis have shaped the upcoming invasion of Iraq and the imposition of sanctions?

Extract 5.2

IRAQ WATER TREATMENT VULNERABILITIES (U)

Filename: 511rept.91

Dtg: 221900z Jan 91

Fm: Dia Washington Dc

Via: Nmist Net

To: Centcom

Info: Centaf

     Uk Strike Command

     Marcent

     18 Abc

     Navcent

     Soccent

     7th Corps

     Ankara

Subject: Iraq Water Treatment Vulnerabilities (U) As Of 18 Jan 91 Key Judgments.

1. Iraq Depends On Importing Specialized Equipment And Some Chemicals To Purify Its Water Supply, Most Of Which Is Heavily Mineralized And Frequently Brackish To Saline.

    ...

2. Failing To Secure Supplies Will Result In A Shortage Of Pure Drinking Water For Much Of The Population. This Could Lead To Increased Incidences, If Not Epidemics, Of Disease And To Certain Pure-Water-Dependent Industries Becoming Incapacitated, Including Petro Chemicals, Fertilizers, Petroleum Refining, Electronics, Pharmaceuticals, Food Processing, Textiles, Concrete Construction, And Thermal Powerplants.

...

5. Unless Water Treatment Supplies Are Exempted From The UN Sanctions For Humanitarian Reasons, No Adequate Solution Exists For Iraq's Water Purification Dilemma, Since No Suitable Alternatives, Including Looting Supplies From Kuwait, Sufficiently Meet Iraqi Needs.

...

11. Iraq's Rivers Also Contain Biological Materials, Pollutants, And Are Laden With Bacteria. Unless The Water Is Purified With Chlorine Epidemics Of Such Diseases As Cholera, Hepatitis, And Typhoid Could Occur.

...

14. ... Recent Reports Indicate The Chlorine Supply Is Critically Low. Its Importation Has Been Embargoed, And Both Main Production Plants Either Had Been Shut Down For A Time Or Have Been Producing Minimal Outputs Because Of The Lack Of Imported Chemicals And The Inability To Replace Parts. ...

...

20. ... Iraq Could Try Convincing The United Nations Or Individual Countries To Exempt Water Treatment Supplies From Sanctions For Humanitarian Reasons. It Probably Also Is Attempting To Purchase Supplies By Using Some Sympathetic Countries As Fronts. If Such Attempts Fail, Iraqi Alternatives Are Not Adequate For Their National Requirements.

...

27. Iraq Will Suffer Increasing Shortages Of Purified Water Because Of The Lack Of Required Chemicals And Desalinization Membranes. Incidences Of Disease, Including Possible Epidemics, Will Become Probable Unless The Population Were Careful To Boil Water Before Consumption, Particularly Since The Sewage Treatment System, Never A High Priority, Will Suffer The Same Loss Of Capability With The Lack Of Chlorine. Locally Produced Food And Medicine Could Be Contaminated. Lack Of Coagulation Chemicals Will Cause

Periodic Shutdowns Of Treatment Plants For Unclogging And
Cleaning Filters, Causing Interruptions Of Water Supplies. As
Desalinization Equipment Becomes Inoperable, Saline Water Sources
Will Become Increasingly Unusable. Temporary Or Permanent Shut
Downs Of Industrial Plants That Rely On Treated Water Will
Multiply. Cannibalizing Lower Priority Operations Will Accelerate
The Trend.

28. ... Full Degradation Of The Water Treatment System Probably Will
Take At Least Another 6 Months.

DIA, 1991

Comment

The document clearly predicted the impact of any decline in water
treatment and sewerage facilities in Iraq and could have been used to
minimise casualties, change the conduct of the war, or plan
reconstruction – in other words to protect civilians in a conflict
situation. However, Nagy (2001) argues that another declassified DIA
document produced in November 1991 suggested the issue for the DIA
was 'public relations' not 'public health', claiming that the main issue
for the USA was that the Iraqi government was continuing to 'exploit
disease incidence data for its own political purposes', despite noting that
public health in Iraq was a 'dominant international concern'. In other
words, the priority for the DIA was not to deal with the public health
issue but prevent the Iraqi government from exploiting the situation to
garner support.

Whatever the purpose, civilians and civilian infrastructure are
increasingly, whether by design or default, becoming caught up in conflict
and war to the extent that the pursuit of national security as currently
understood is having fundamental implications for human security.

2.3 International law, public health and human security

Attempts have been made through international agreements and
conventions to respond to the challenges discussed in the previous
section and here we consider one of them. Chapter 1 introduced the
concept of juridification – broadly meaning the attempt to bring an
increasing number of social problems within a regulatory or legal
framework – and some of the dilemmas of juridification were explored
in Chapter 4. On the one hand, the extent to which the juridification
process has the potential to define new rights for and extend protections
to previously excluded or disadvantaged social groups represents positive

possibilities. But its largely symbolic function also means that it has the potential to create and institutionalise injustices, protecting already privileged groups and reducing possibilities of democratic accountability. The framework of international law as it regulates behaviour towards civilians in the course of war is another context in which these dilemmas are apparent.

The Geneva Convention of 12 August 1949, designed to protect prisoners of war and proscribe the conduct of war, was further enhanced by a series of Protocols, one of which – Protocol 1 adopted on 8 June 1977 by the Diplomatic Conference on the Reaffirmation and Development of International Humanitarian Law applicable in Armed Conflicts, and coming into force on 7 December 1979 – related to the 'Protection of Victims of International Armed Conflicts' (OHCHR, 2008). The Protocol has created certain ambiguities, however. While Article 54(2) states that it is 'prohibited to attack, destroy, remove or render useless objects indispensable to the survival of the civilian population, such as foodstuffs, agricultural areas for the production of foodstuffs, crops, livestock, drinking water installations and supplies and irrigation works', if military planners can demonstrate in particular circumstances that these support military capacities – in other words, that they are 'dual use' – they can be treated as a legitimate target in law (Smith, 2002).

Activity 5.4

Consider these provisions in the Protocol. What effect might this be expected to have on the targeting of infrastructural assets in war, as discussed in Sections 2.1 and 2.2?

Comment

In some respects the Protocol seems quite unequivocal and would appear to outlaw many of the military tactics identified by Graham. However, there are two qualifications which need to be made before drawing such a conclusion. The first is to do with the notion of 'dual use'. This is quite a significant qualification since facilities are rarely simply used by civilians, even if their predominant use is civilian.

The second qualification goes to the heart of attempts to juridify social – and in this case international – relations. While a convention such as the Geneva Convention may have a significant moral authority and even a broadly legal authority, its relevance can only ultimately be confirmed either if it shapes behaviour or if it can be enforced in practice. This particular Protocol – even with the level of permissiveness implied by the notion of 'dual use' – proved controversial for some states, including China, Israel and the USA. The USA, for example, signed the Protocol on 12 December 1977 but it was never ratified in the US Senate. Indeed, in 1987 President Reagan censured Protocol 1 around fears that it was 'pro-terrorist', because it attempted to extend Geneva Convention protections to combatants of 'liberation struggles'. This particularly related to suggestions that it would allow Palestinian Liberation Organization members to claim prisoner of war status (Meron, 1994).

Such difficulties around international law reflect some of the problems associated with attempts to juridify international conflict and war, and, specifically, the formulation of legal protections but without effective forms of sanction. Similar issues arise from the wider debate around national security and protection from external threats. In the case of the Iraq war initiated by the USA and the UK in 2003, for example, the core justifications were couched in terms of notions of pre-emptive action or preventative war, emphasising either the potential terrorist threat posed by the Iraqi regime or their access to 'weapons of mass destruction' (both never proven). These justifications have been substantially questioned by those who see them as running counter to the framework of international law that seeks to prescribe the conditions around which war can be initiated; that is, national defence. The juridification of war through international legal frameworks, in the case of Iraq, did not stop the war, but it did provide an uneasy debate around what was legally acceptable (see Roberts, 2003) and ultimately may be said to have contributed to problems of legitimacy for both the US and UK governments.

The existence of this Protocol and the Geneva Convention itself provides a context within which debates about the behaviour of states and other agencies can be placed. They help to provide a benchmark against which that behaviour may be judged. Part of the human security agenda is the placing of human priorities against those of states, so that public health agendas may be considered within the terms of war. Macqueen et al. (2004) make this case and argue that public health practitioners should aim to address the causes of disease, work to prevent it, and attempt to empower the disenfranchised to access resources and health care. It is obvious, they maintain, that the conditions of war create difficult social problems and that in time of war no government can necessarily extend the same levels of care given to their own citizens to those of other nations. However, in their discussion of the position in Iraq after the 2003 invasion, they suggest that:

> [N]either the government of the United States nor any other government should knowingly prevent the government of Iraq from acting according to these principles [of public health]. We believe that this extension of public health principles is valid even if the government of the second state (Iraq in this case) is deficient in its own adherence to the principles of public health.
>
> (Macqueen et al., 2004, p. 112)

These debates indicate some of the conflicts between national and human security. From the national security perspective, 'rogue states' should be dealt with by force, and civilian casualties are merely an unfortunate and unavoidable consequence of war. From the human security perspective, it is argued that, even in extreme situations such as war, protections can and should be extended to civilians, which, in the long term, offers more hope for reconstruction and peace in post-conflict situations.

3   Trying to deliver human security: managing health and disease

So far, we have focused on a policy area that has only recently influenced the ways in which social policy or criminology are generally conceptualised. However, we hope that we have shown how focusing on these issues helps to confirm the uneasy relationship between attempts to deliver forms of security and the experience of people having to live with the consequences. We have also sought to highlight some of the ways in which attempts have been made to manage and regulate war and conflict, as well as the tensions between attempts to protect civilians while pursuing military ambitions. In this section we turn to health, which is a much more familiar area of social policy, and set out to consider the difference it makes to begin to frame questions of health internationally or globally, and not just in national terms.

3.1 Health as a global issue

Historically, health has been seen as an issue for national policy – the UK has a National Health Service and other countries similarly have their own quite distinctive health regimes. From this perspective, it is the health of national populations that needs to be protected. However, as illustrated by the establishment of the World Health Organization (WHO) in 1948, health is also viewed as a global concern. Why is this?

There are three widely stated justifications for taking a broader – globalised – view of health and disease as an object of policy. The first is the moral argument – the need to alleviate human suffering as an object of any civilised global system of governance. The second is that the scale of the task is such that the major health needs of people in poorer countries cannot be met without external support. And the third is that infectious disease is no respecter of national boundaries and if something is not done about the problems faced in poorer countries then they will soon also be problems in the richer countries. As Keil and Ali (2006, p. 108) put it, 'the geography of globalization is a geography of disease'. The combination of moral imperative (which emphasises the need to provide support to the populations most at risk) and enlightened self-interest (for agencies in the richer countries) has been summed up in the comments of Nils Daulaire, President and CEO of the Global Health Council:

> [M]ost of us in health professions have a simple response to the question of why we engage in global health: because it is right to help those who are sick and in need, and because this is at the heart of our calling … But there exists an argument beyond the moral and humanitarian aspects of global health. In a changing and dangerous world, United States engagement in global health has emerged as a fundamental national interest.
>
> (quoted in Lee and Collin, 2005, p. 151)

The management of global disease is therefore increasingly identified as a security concern for all nations. In terms of the manifesto for human security we considered in Section 1, the control and prevention of disease is identified as being essential for human development. However, such concerns also powerfully combine with the idea of national security. The implication is that policies aimed at reducing the incidence of disease in poorer countries and improving the health of their residents will have the additional benefit of reducing the threat of disease to richer countries. But there may also be threats which fit more directly within the national security paradigm. Lee and Collin (2005, p. 157), for example, note that the threat of 'state instability and failure … caused by HIV/AIDS, in both sub-Saharan Africa and other regions of strategic importance, is a key argument' in persuading policymakers in the richer countries of the world (and particularly the USA) of the need to tackle the HIV/AIDS epidemics in poorer countries of the world.

Health and disease are today often approached through a narrow medical lens. When we are ill we go to the doctor who provides us with medicines intended to cure us, even if some of us may also be told that we should pursue healthier lifestyles, take more exercise, drink less alcohol, give up smoking and eat more fruit. The great public health initiatives of the nineteenth and twentieth centuries, associated with slum clearance and the development of effective urban sanitation and sewerage, highlighted different issues. As Gandy (2003, p. 37) notes, 'The historical synergy between health reform and social justice has been displaced by an increasing emphasis on the individual patient (or consumer) rather than the wider social and political context for disease'.

Nevertheless, it is increasingly clear that any attempt to understand the spread of disease (bacterial infection and viruses) also has to be located within social and economic contexts. This is the focus of social epidemiology – that is, the study of the ways in which disease affects particular populations and what it is that influences the distribution of disease between them. Social epidemiologists have identified a series of factors that might be relevant in different cases. These include economic change, war and famine, agriculture, the global movement of peoples and goods, global warming and the implosion of national and global public health regimes (see Morse, 1993). What these studies have shown is that the potential for the emergence of new diseases through mutation or the re-emergence of old but increasingly resistant strains has been increased as a result of alterations in human behaviour resulting from economic, social and environmental change. Gandy (2005, p. 10) argues forcibly that 'If we are to make sense of the current public health crisis, we need to explore interconnections between political, economic and social developments that are ignored by the fragmentary emphasis of the biomedical sciences'.

This can be illustrated through the case of pandemic influenza, which has been, and may still be, a significant threat to both national and human security (a pandemic is a 'new' infectious disease whose incidence spreads across a wide geographical area and affects a very high proportion of the population, because people have little natural immunity). The dramatic impact of pandemic influenza on Europe and the USA following the First World War in 1918, when tens of millions of people died, has served as a warning for the contemporary era. The issue seems to be not whether there will be another such event, but when it will take place, and how it will be managed. Although, at the time of writing in late 2007, the level of popular concern about it has receded, the example of avian influenza illustrates the complex process of interaction between health, socio-economic position, rapid social change, punitive public policy and disease. In his analysis of its spread (drawing on a wide range of literature) in South East Asia, Davis (2005) argues that a combination of economic change, the power of big business and the weakness or corruption of governments has influenced the pattern of disease. Similar points have been made about the return of tuberculosis as a disease that is widespread mainly in the poorer countries of the world, but also liable to erupt in the cities generally thought of as wealthy, such as New York in the early 1990s (Gandy and Zumla, 2003).

In the next section, we explore the relationship between social and economic factors and the spread and management of disease, with the help of a discussion of the case of HIV/AIDS.

3.2 The social context of HIV/AIDS as a global health crisis

HIV (or human immunodeficiency virus) weakens and damages the body's immune system, so that it is unable to fight off common infections. As the charity FPA explains in a leaflet prepared for the British National Health Service, 'Someone who has HIV is diagnosed as having AIDS [acquired immune deficiency syndrome] only when ... their immune system has been badly damaged and they develop particular illnesses. These are known as AIDS-defining illnesses, and include recurrent pneumonia and tuberculosis' (FPA, 2007, p. 3). Even if untreated, it may take several years before someone diagnosed with HIV develops the symptoms of AIDS.

Globally, the impact of HIV/AIDS has a distinctive pattern, with significant concentrations of people with HIV in southern Africa, as well as some of the countries of South East Asia and the Caribbean (see Figure 5.8). Around 70 per cent of those with HIV/AIDS live in Africa. It is widely accepted that where HIV/AIDS reaches epidemic proportions it brings other economic, social and cultural disasters in its wake. As one WHO report explains:

> Globally, HIV/AIDS epidemics are already having a disastrous domino effect. Millions of children are orphaned, communities are destroyed, health services are overwhelmed, entire countries face hunger and economic ruin.
>
> ...
>
> Large-scale negative changes to patterns of economic and social behaviour are likely to result from the epidemic's impact on population structure and adult life expectancy. Beyond the loss of income and the diversion of income to health expenditures, families resort to various 'coping' strategies with negative long-term effects, including migration, child labour, sale of assets and spending of savings. Families suffering from the illness or death of one or more of their members experience both the direct costs of medical and funeral expenditures and the indirect costs of the impact of the illness on productivity.
>
> HIV/AIDS is changing the very structure of populations. There are increased dependency ratios in many African countries, for example, with smaller numbers of working-age adults on whom both children and elderly relatives depend; a situation that is becoming more severe.
>
> The psychological effects on young people of seeing their immediate elders dying in huge numbers at such young ages, and consequent fears for their own future, are immense and will have profound effects on economic development. Moreover, as parents (most of the young adults) die prematurely, they fail to hand on assets and skills to their children. In this way, HIV/AIDS weakens the process through which human capital – people's experience, skill and knowledge – is accumulated and transmitted across generations.
>
> (WHO, 2004, p. 8)

These are powerful insights and the negative impact of HIV/AIDS on social and economic development cannot be denied. HIV/AIDS is identified by de Waal (2003, p. 125) as 'a critical and pervasive threat to human security, like no other', because it bears directly on the possibilities of human development, reflected in mortality rates, and low life expectancy, to the extent that in sub-Saharan Africa, adult life expectancy has been reduced by about twenty years. 'The direct impact of HIV,' he continues, 'namely the death of tens of millions of human beings from AIDS – is the greatest threat to human life in the coming century' (de Waal, 2003, p. 126).

It is widely accepted that there is a global health crisis of HIV/AIDS and there is a recurrent fear of its resurgence (e.g. via the countries of the former Soviet Union) in the countries of the West and North where it currently seems largely to be under control. Finding ways of tackling the crisis, however, has proved rather more difficult.

The dominant view of HIV/AIDS is filtered through an emphasis on its transmission as a result of sexual activity, or (to a lesser extent) on the dangers of drug injecting with shared needles. According to the World Health Organization, HIV/AIDS is transmitted mainly by sexual intercourse between men and women in southern Africa and through 'drug injecting and commercial sex networks' in the countries of Asia (WHO, 2004, p. 3). This understanding focuses on the way in which the virus is spread, and, of course, accurately reflects that process. However, because, from this perspective, the spread of HIV/AIDS is seen as a function of biological transmission through sexual and other behaviour,

Figure 5.7

Promoting abstinence in the fight against AIDS in Uganda

the solution in turn is largely identified as one of prevention through the regulation in one form or another of sexual conduct. The *prevention* of transmission is encouraged, whether through sexual abstinence, the use of prophylaxes such as condoms, or the avoidance of intravenous drug taking (or through needle-sharing schemes). We can also see here that this strategy is a *responsibilising* one, where individuals are given the responsibility of altering their personal conduct.

Stillwaggon (2005), however, argues that the spread of HIV/AIDS is closely associated with the incidence of poverty, particularly malnutrition, parasitic diseases, malaria and poor health care. She notes that the nature of the epidemic and its spread in richer and poorer countries of the world has been quite different, with far higher levels and rates of growth in the latter than the former. In the case of Africa (which is often treated as an undifferentiated whole in the literature of AIDS prevention), for example, high levels of HIV/AIDS have been explained largely in terms of differences in sexual behaviour, despite such an assumption depending 'on epic rates of sexual partner change ... for which empirical support is lacking' (Stillwaggon, 2005, p. 134). Stillwaggon charts the way in which particular stereotypes of sexual behaviour have been translated into public policy, with little critical attention to the supposed evidence: 'What distinguishes most Africans, Asians, and Latin Americans from most Europeans and North Americans is not extraordinary behaviour but poverty. Effective prevention depends on recognizing the real commonalities among people, as well as the real differences' (Stillwaggon, 2005, p. 157).

Figure 5.8
HIV prevalence. Territory size shows the proportion of all people aged 15–49 with HIV worldwide, living there (Source: Worldmapper Map 227)

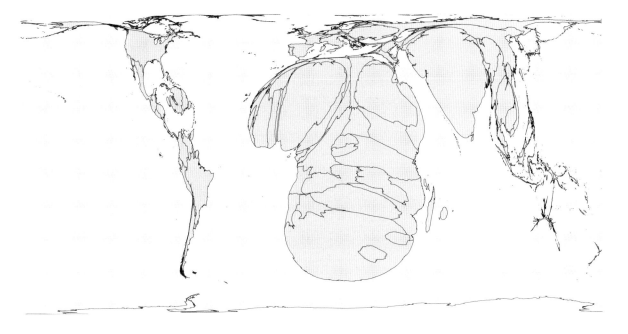

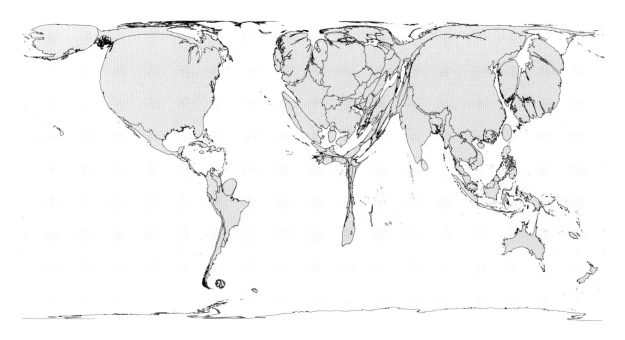

Figure 5.9

Women's income. Territory size shows the proportion of worldwide women's income earned there, measured by local purchasing power. The picture for men's income calculated on the same basis is similar, but average levels are higher and the Indian subcontinent is represented as significantly larger (in other words, the gap between men's and women's earnings is greater than in comparable parts of the world). Income levels have been used as a measure of poverty, rather than global poverty indices, because of the difficulties of calculating these on a global scale (Source: Worldmapper Map 147)

Activity 5.5

Look at the global maps of poverty and the incidence of HIV/AIDS in Figures 5.8 and 5.9 and compare them. Can you identify any common patterns? To what extent, if at all, does this help in assessing the direction of the causal relationship between poverty and HIV/AIDS? In other words, to what extent does it help in identifying whether poverty is a consequence of the high incidence of HIV/AIDS or a high incidence of HIV/AIDS a consequence of poverty? What further information would help you to determine the nature of the relationship?

Comment

This representation of the data is consistent with the points made by Stillwaggon, since the places with higher levels of poverty are also those with greater incidence of HIV. However, that does not necessarily, in itself, prove that there is a direct causal relationship. Indeed, it could equally be consistent with the view that it is HIV/AIDS that has caused the greater incidence of poverty in these countries. All that is proven in these figures is that there is a correlation between HIV/AIDS and poverty – meaning that they are both found in the same areas but we don't yet know what causal relationship exists between them.

This highlights the importance of the ways in which evidence is interpreted. This evidence of the transmission process is real enough. However, it does not necessarily explain why the incidence of HIV/AIDS varies so much between countries. As Stillwaggon emphasises, it would only do so if one could assume implausibly huge differences in behaviour between those countries. Instead, she forcibly draws our attention to a different sort of evidence, namely the relationship between the incidence of HIV/AIDS and poverty. Stillwaggon argues that the differences can best be explained by the levels and forms of poverty in countries where HIV/AIDS is endemic. One reason why this might be the case lies, for example, in the extent to which malnutrition lowers immunity to disease.

In taking this debate further, it would be important to chart the changing patterns of poverty in these countries – in other words, if they were already poor before the rise of the HIV/AIDS epidemic, that would suggest that the social context was important. The approach adopted by Stillwagon and others has been sharply criticised by those who argue that it oversimplifies the impact of poverty – since, for example, the incidence of HIV/AIDS in many African countries is higher among better off households than poorer ones (see, for example, Pisani, 2008). If there were examples of significant differences between countries which began with similar levels of poverty and whose populations had markedly different styles of sexual behaviour, then clearly it would be important to place more emphasis on finding ways of changing behaviour.

The implications of acknowledging the social and economic context which underlies the spread of the disease suggest that solely targeting HIV/AIDS through medical intervention and drives to behavioural modification (however important that may be) are unlikely to be wholly successful in substantially reducing its incidence. Those sorts of policies may help to keep things under control – isolated and under surveillance – so that those living in richer countries are protected, but it is only wider strategies capable of challenging poverty that offer the prospect of reducing the differences between the national incidence of HIV/AIDS. Similarly, however, poverty alleviation strategies in themselves are unlikely to be effective in tackling the problem of HIV/AIDS.

So far, we have not discussed other forms of medical treatment, through a range of drugs, which have been shown to be effective in the world's richer countries. Clearly, making such drugs available at reasonable cost in countries or areas with higher poverty levels could have a significant impact on HIV/AIDS, but here, too, the economic and social context cannot be ignored. The uneven ways in which such treatment is available across the world also highlights the divisions between poorer and richer countries and, indeed, between poorer and richer populations within countries. It is more difficult to deliver effective long-term treatment to individuals in some social contexts (and some communities) than others, and the investment in the required medical infrastructure also tends to be lower in poorer than richer countries. These are certainly insights that are identifiable within the human security paradigm.

The difficulty created by the way in which the pragmatic management of disease has become bound up in economic and political contexts and conflicts means that particular populations are identified as being at risk of disease, and policies that are developed tend to be both aimed at protecting them (curing them, vaccinating them, etc.) and at containing the 'threat' they seem to represent (demonising them, blaming them, restricting their movement, etc.). This approach reflects the 'national security' paradigm, emphasising national protection and defence against the broader global interest. Therefore, in the case of HIV/AIDS, for example, emphasis is placed on the inappropriateness (and dangerousness) of people's sexual behaviour, particularly in poorer countries. The slip from being identified as being at risk to being risky – threatening others and their security – is particularly easy to see in this context, and as such security concerns become focused on finding ways to contain the threat posed by poorer nations or continents (Feldbaum et al., 2006).

The challenge for social scientists and others looking for policy-relevant evidence in this context is that what is needed is likely to involve an approach that brings together the different aspects of the process. Strategies orientated towards dealing with individual cases (changing behaviour or – possibly more important – providing medical support to those suffering from HIV/AIDS) will need to be combined with strategies that are effectively targeted on the reduction of poverty. If, as Blanc and Uplekar (2003, p. 106) suggest in the case of TB, there is a process of 'reciprocal causation' (in which poverty makes the incidence of HIV/AIDS more likely and higher levels of HIV/AIDS increase the likelihood of poverty for those who suffer from it and for the countries in which they live), then the strategies needed to tackle HIV/AIDS will have to both target poverty and provide appropriate medical care.

3.3 The global management of disease

The discussion in the previous section has focused on just one of the major global health issues that present challenges for policymakers. This section looks at some of the institutional arrangements which have emerged in response to some of these challenges.

The management of health in a global setting is overseen by the World Health Organization (WHO), which was set up to coordinate the management of disease and the maintenance of public health and preventative regimes (WHO, 2006). The WHO has responsibility for the management of the International Health Regulations (IHR), an international treaty first agreed between the WHO's members in 1969. These regulations have historically required member states to notify the WHO about the incidence of a particular set of infectious diseases (cholera, plague, yellow fever and smallpox – until its global eradication). These regulations were renegotiated in 2005 to extend the list of notifiable diseases, diseases that had been growing at a rate of about one a year for the previous twenty years (Merianos and Peiris, 2005). There was also concern that individual national governments might be reluctant to notify the WHO about the incidence of particular diseases because such notification might quickly lead to trade and travel restrictions; this was said to underpin China's reluctance to confirm the outbreak of SARS (severe acute respiratory syndrome), another potential epidemic, in 2002, until the following year when it had already been spread more widely.

Since 2007, when the new regulations came into force, members have to notify the WHO of 'all events which may constitute a public health emergency of international concern' (WHO, 2005, Part II, Article 6(1)). Under the regulations individual states continued to have prime responsibility and were expected to develop surveillance facilities capable of identifying potentially serious outbreaks. However, since 2007 the WHO has had the responsibility to assist those countries with limited resources and – equally significant – has also had the facility to call on a wider range of sources to identify the emergence of such outbreaks, and can itself identify an emergency, even where a particular state has not done so.

The emphasis of the regulations was clearly on the risk of the international spread of disease and the impact this might have on international trade (Merianos and Peiris, 2005). This illustrated that in many ways the concern was to provide measures to prevent infectious diseases ravaging developing nations from encroaching on the affluent West, rather than attempt to resolve disease and other associated social problems at source. So, for example, in December 2005 the US Congress allocated $3.8 billion to help prepare for the next influenza pandemic, of which $3.3 was allocated to the Department of Health and Human Services. Most of this was to be spent on the stockpiling of antiviral drugs and vaccines for use in the USA, with only 3.8 per cent being dedicated to international activities. As one PLoS (Public Library of Science) editorial argued:

> Poor countries are understandably concerned that the stockpiling of tools for pandemic influenza control will be the preserve of the rich world.
>
> ... The woolly language of IHR 2005 also leaves the regulations open to the criticism that they are there simply to prevent infectious diseases of the poor world from encroaching upon rich countries.
>
> (*PLoS Medicine* Editors, 2007, p. 5)

Like the forms of juridification discussed in Section 2.3 of this chapter, the extent to which an effective global regime can be constructed remains uncertain, and for similar reasons. Although the IHR gives the WHO a degree of autonomy and some authority in identifying public health risks, it remains an international treaty between the members of the WHO. This means that those members continue to be able to determine how well the regulations work and WHO's authority over them remains contested. A series of other obstacles to the success of constructing an effective global public health regime has also been identified. There are technical obstacles – pathogens may present in unusual ways, which makes it difficult to assess their significance or even to detect them at an early stage; resources are also likely to be a problem, particularly for poorer countries, and the WHO does not have the funds to overcome this; in some countries (particularly federal states), agreement at national level through a treaty of this sort may still face legal difficulties; and politically there is still no guarantee that states will act according to the priorities of global health policy, since they may be disadvantaged through trade and travel restrictions if they do (Baker and Fidler, 2006). The weaknesses of global public health regimes have obvious implications for relations between developing and developed nations, and for the choice between protection and punitivity. In the absence of resources to provide health care, sanitation and poverty alleviation, the default response to disease control can often be exclusion, whether expressed as population control or attempts to insulate the effects of disease in developing nations through border controls (Yeates, 2001).

4   Review

Throughout this chapter we have explored the tensions between two different paradigms or ways of thinking; that is, between human and national security. These two paradigms represent, at a global and institutional level, the core concerns of this book – the competing logics of welfare and crime control – and how the concept and pursuit of security has reconfigured these relationships. We have considered how these two apparently competing logics interact in two case studies: first, we looked at how contemporary conceptions of national security are pursued through preventative and punitive war, and how this has implications for the welfare and protection (or lack of protection) of people in conflict situations; second, we looked at the emergence of global welfare policy on health and disease, considering the necessity of understanding some of the social dynamics behind the spread of disease. We also explored some of the ways in which a range of institutional arrangements have been created to try to manage the uneasy relationships implied by these competing logics.

Throughout the chapter, we have used a range of evidence to inform and elaborate the arguments. We have been particularly interested in the ways in which evidence may feed into policy development, and this was relevant to the discussion around Activities 5.3 (relating to water supplies in Iraq) and 5.5 (relating to the management of HIV/AIDS). In the case of the former, the relatively dry report leaves policymakers to determine what use they want to make of the findings – they may mobilise them either with a focus on national security (or military strategy) or to find some means of ensuring that populations are protected from the impact of military action (if the emphasis is placed on human security). In the case of the latter, the debate is important because it suggests the need to develop different approaches to policy – a shift away from seeing the problem solely in terms of disease transmission (which encourages both a moral agenda of responsibilisation and an emphasis on the managing of populations to ensure that the healthy are protected behind effective border controls) towards one that stresses the need to see it as a wider global social and economic challenge, relating to issues of social justice (see **Newman and Yeates, 2008a**), which broadly represents the human security agenda.

Although the two approaches which frame the chapter seem to be competing in some respects, it is also important to recognise the extent to which they are entangled together in practice. This can be seen in the process of juridification that has been explored in this chapter and throughout the book. The extension of human rights and international law may do much to draw symbolic boundaries around the conduct of major powers, but has seemingly not yet managed to make serious inroads into policy and practice. As a result, human security agendas have also been harnessed to more traditional security concerns. The pursuit of human security may enhance national security, since challenging poverty and the human consequences of war and conflict may impact positively on terrorism and extremism. Similarly, the notion of human security may be mobilised to support forms of military intervention which have the aim of reducing conflict within a particular territory (imposing peace) or of providing support to some disadvantaged or oppressed population within a country (Wood and Shearing, 2006, pp. 77–9). In other words, the search for human security may slip over into, or provide a justification for, punitive intervention. As this book has examined in many different contexts, the emphasis on security as a concept which underpins human development and social order has created new entanglements between the logics of welfare and crime control. The following, final, chapter returns to this entanglement.

Further reading

For a comprehensive discussion of the social epidemiology of war, you may find it interesting to read *War and Public Health*, edited by Barry Levy and Victor Sidel (2005, Oxford University Press). *The Monster at Our Door: The Global Threat of Avian Flu* by Mike Davis (2005, The New Press) provides an engaging sociological account of the emergence of avian influenza as a global threat. Eileen Stillwaggon's *Aids and the Ecology of Poverty* (2005, Oxford University Press) is a fascinating review of the relationship between AIDS and global poverty.

References

Baker, M. and Fidler, D. (2006) 'Global public health surveillance under new international health regulations', *Emerging Infectious Diseases*, vol. 12, no. 7, pp. 1058–65.

Blanc, L. and Uplekar, M. (2003) 'The present global burden of tuberculosis' in Gandy and Zumla (eds) (2003).

Care International/Johns Hopkins University Center for International Emergency, Disaster and Refugee Studies (2003) *Humanitarian Assistance Capacity in Iraq: Part 1*, London and Baltimore, MD, Care International/Johns Hopkins University.

Chen, L. and Narasimhan, V. (2003) 'A human security agenda for public health' in Chen, L., Learning, J. and Narasimhan, V. (eds) *Global Health Challenges for Human Security*, Cambridge, MA, Harvard University Press.

Cochrane, A. and Walters, R. (2008) 'The globalisation of social justice' in Newman and Yeates (eds) (2008b).

Commission on Human Security (2003a) *Outline of the Report of the Commission on Human Security* [online], http://www.humansecurity-chs.org/finalreport/ Outlines/outline.html (Accessed 23 January 2008).

Commission on Human Security (2003b) *Human Security Now*, New York, NY, Commission on Human Security.

Davis, M. (2005) *The Monster at Our Door: The Global Threat of Avian Flu*, New York, NY, The New Press.

de Waal, A. (2003) 'HIV/AIDS: the security issue of a lifetime' in Chen, L., Leaning, J. and Narasimhan, V. (eds) *Global Health Challenges for Human Security*, Cambridge, MA, Harvard University Press.

Defence Intelligence Agency (DIA) (1991) 'Iraq water treatment vulnerabilities' [online] http://www.gulflink.osd.mil/declassdocs/dia/19950901/ 950901_511rept_91.html (Accessed 12 December 2007).

Family Planning Association (FPA) (2007) *HIV: Looking After Your Sexual Health*, London, FPA.

Feldbaum, H., Patel, P., Sondorp, E. and Lee, K. (2006) 'Global health and national security: the need for critical engagement', *Medicine, Conflict and Survival*, vol. 22, no. 3, pp. 192–8.

FitzSimons, D.W. and Whiteside, A.W. (1994) 'Conflict, war and public health', *Conflict Studies 276*, Nov/Dec.

Gandy, M. (2003) 'Life without germs' in Gandy and Zumla (eds) (2003).

Gandy, M. (2005) 'Deadly alliances: death, disease, and the global politics of public health', *PLoS Medicine*, vol. 2, no. 1, e4, pp. 9–11.

Gandy, M. and Zumla, A. (eds) (2003) *The Return of the White Plague: Global Poverty and the 'New' Tuberculosis*, London, Verso.

Garfield, R.M. and Neugut, A.I. (1997) 'The human consequences of war' in Levy and Sidel (eds) (1997b).

Graham, S. (2005) 'Switching cities off: urban infrastructure and US air power', *City*, vol. 9, no. 2, pp. 169–94.

Graham, S. (2006) 'Cities and the "war on terror"', *International Journal of Urban and Regional Research*, vol. 30, no. 2, pp. 255–76.

Keil, R. and Ali, H. (2006) 'The avian flu: some lessons learned from the 2003 SARS outbreak in Toronto', *Area*, vol. 38, no. 1, pp. 107–9.

King, G. and Martin, L.L. (2001) 'Overview paper: the human costs of military conflict', *Military Conflict as a Public Health Problem*, 29 September.

Lee, K. and Collin, J. (eds) (2005) *Global Change and Health*, Maidenhead, Open University Press.

Levy, B.S. and Sidel, V.W. (1997a) 'The impact of military activities on civilian populations' in Levy and Sidel (eds) (1997b).

Levy, B.S. and Sidel, V.W. (eds) (1997b) *War and Public Health,* Oxford, Oxford University Press.

Macqueen, G., Nagy, T., Barbera, J.S. and Raichle, C. (2004) 'Iraq water treatment vulnerabilities: a challenge to public health ethics', *Medicine, Conflict and Survival*, vol. 20, no. 2, pp. 109–19.

Merianos, A. and Peiris, M. (2005) 'International Health Regulations (2005)', *The Lancet*, no. 366, 8 October, pp. 1249–51.

Meron, T. (1994) 'The time has come for the United States to ratify Geneva Protocol I', *The American Journal of International Law*, vol. 88, no. 4, pp. 678–86.

Morse, S. (ed.) (1993) *Emerging Viruses*, Oxford, Oxford University Press.

Nagy, T.J. (2001) 'How the US deliberately destroyed Iraq's water' [online], www.globalresearch.ca/articles/NAG108A.html (Accessed 29 June 2007).

Newman, J. and Yeates, N. (2008a) 'Making social justice: ideas, struggles and responses' in Newman and Yeates (eds) (2008b).

Newman, J. and Yeates, N. (eds) (2008b) *Social Justice: Welfare, Crime and Society*, Maidenhead, Open University Press/Milton Keynes, The Open University.

Office of the High Commissioner for Human Rights (OHCHR) (2008) *Protocol Additional to the Geneva Conventions of 12 August 1949, and Relating to the Protection of Victims of International Armed Conflicts (Protocol 1)* [online], Geneva, United Nations, http://www2.ohcr.org/english/law/protocol1.htm (Accessed 10 March 2008).

Pisani, E. (2008) *The Wisdom of Whores: Bureaucrats, Brothels and the Business of Aids*, London, Granta.

PLoS Medicine Editors (2007) 'How is WHO responding to global public health threats?', *PLoS Medicine*, vol. 4, no. 5, e197.

Reigle, D.A. and D'Amato, A.M. (1994) *US Chemical and Biological Warfare – Related Dual Use Exports to Iraq and their Possible Impact on the Health Consequences of the Gulf War,* Washington, DC, Committee on Banking, Housing & Urban Affairs with Respect to Export Administration.

Roberts, A. (2003) 'The law and the use of force after Iraq', *Survival*, vol. 45, no. 2, pp. 31–56.

Smith, T.W. (2002) 'The new law of war: legitimising hi-tech and infrastructural violence', *International Studies Quarterly*, vol. 46, pp. 355–74.

Stillwaggon, E. (2005) *Aids and the Ecology of Poverty*, Oxford, Oxford University Press.

United Nations Development Programme (UNDP) (1994) *Human Development Report 1994*, New York, NY, United Nations Development Programme.

United Nations Population Fund (UNFPA) (2007) *State of the World Population 2007*: *Unleashing the Potential of Urban Growth*, New York, NY, United Nations Population Fund.

Wood, J. and Shearing, C. (2006) *Imagining Security*, Uffculme, Willan.

World Health Organization (WHO) (2004) *The World Health Report 2004: Changing History*, Geneva, World Health Organization.

World Health Organization (WHO) (2005) *International Health Regulations*, Geneva, World Health Organization.

World Health Organization (WHO) (2006) *Working for Health: An Introduction to the World Health Organization*, Geneva, World Health Organization.

Yeates, N. (2001) *Globalization and Social Policy*, London, Sage.

Chapter 6
Conclusion

Allan Cochrane and Deborah Talbot

Contents

1 Revisiting the questions about security

Throughout this book, its chapters have examined how insecurity and the search for security are reflected in the interrelationships and entanglements of welfare policy and crime control. In the 'Introduction' to Chapter 1, we set out the following questions:

- Why has security become such an important idea and how does the concept of security link the different domains of social, personal and political life, and especially the worlds of crime control and welfare?

- Why do people and governments invest so much in the pursuit of different forms of security? How might we understand the types of policy and political responses that are generated by the search for security?

- How do we make sense of the changing nature of the relationship between security and insecurity, as expressed in social welfare and crime control policy?

- Why do the measures pursued to provide security often not deliver it – indeed, instead often seem to enhance a sense of insecurity?

We also set out a commitment to explore the ways in which different sorts of evidence may be used to analyse the development of particular policy initiatives and their impact on a range of social groups, and to consider the ways in which evidence is or might be used to inform the process of policymaking.

Activity 6.1

We would like you to think about these questions in the context of the issues which were examined in Chapters 2, 3, 4 and 5. Table 6.1 repeats the questions as column headings, and lists just a few of the issues and policies covered in this book, as row headings. Try to identify, as far as possible, how each of the questions might be answered with the help of the cases identified down the left side of the grid. We have completed the first row and some other grid entries to illustrate how this might be done, but identifying the columns in which to place particular points will not always be straightforward. However, it's more important to use the questions as a means of drawing out the evidence from the chapters than to worry about how it should be divided up between the columns.

While you are working on this activity, you should think about the kinds of evidence that have been used in the chapters to investigate and explore these issues. The chapters of the book also reflect on the ways in which evidence can be used to help us understand how policy is developed, as well as the ways in which it helps to shape and influence policy.

We return in Section 3 to discussing the ways in which evidence can be used, but it would be helpful if you kept these points in mind as you go through this activity. You might wish to ask the same questions of any of the other issues, examples or case studies introduced in the book.

Table 6.1 Answering the questions

	How does the search for security link the different domains of social, personal and political life?	How should the policy and political responses generated by the search for security be understood?	How has the relationship between security and insecurity been expressed in social welfare and crime control policy?	In what ways does the pursuit of security sometimes enhance a sense of insecurity?
Sports utility vehicles (Chapter 2, Section 3.2)	The rise of SUVs directly links social and personal lives: the search for personal (or family) security underpins the search for protected spaces within which security can be taken for granted. In that sense it is a political strategy, because it shapes the way society is organised	Policy responses to the rise of the SUV have been ambiguous. The individual decision to purchase SUVs is increasingly identified as problematic, particularly because of the way in which it threatens the security of others (in crashes) and of us all (through pollution and global warming). However, there has been little direct control on the use of SUVs and in practice urban planning continues to favour road transport	The rise of SUVs has largely been driven by private-sector marketing and individualised responses to social fears, although it also has to be understood in the wider context of the way in which risk has increasingly been privatised, and managing it has become the responsibility of individuals, families and communities (in a process of responsibilisation)	SUVs may help generate security for those driving them, but drivers are also constantly reminded of danger by the mechanisms of protection promoted by the SUV. This means they may also feel more threatened when outside the protection of the SUV. Other road users are, of course, excluded from that protection, and may also face increased risk and insecurity in any collision with an SUV
Safeguarding children (Chapter 3, Section 3)	Families are crucial sites across which the search for security is played out. As social institutions they are often understood to be places of safety for their members, including children. However, particular families may also be experienced as highly insecure by those		Policy interventions have combined rhetorical support for families with direct intervention to protect children and encourage better parenting. The drive has generally been seen as socially protective, but the disciplinary process can also result in	

	How does the search for security link the different domains of social, personal and political life?	How should the policy and political responses generated by the search for security be understood?	How has the relationship between security and insecurity been expressed in social welfare and crime control policy?	In what ways does the pursuit of security sometimes enhance a sense of insecurity?
	suffering forms of abuse or domestic violence. Families are also often understood to be the places within which children are socialised and trained how to behave. Yet, this means that some of them may be identified as failing in this task – producing a generation of disorderly young people		punitive intervention of one sort or another (such as the removal of children from families)	
Hate crime legislation (Chapter 4, Section 3)		The identification of crimes as hate crimes can be seen as an attempt to protect particular populations through the criminal law (linking the processes of juridification and criminalisation), without the need for social expenditure to compensate disadvantaged communities. Hate crime legislation is as important symbolically as it is in terms of any particular judicial intervention		

	How does the search for security link the different domains of social, personal and political life?	How should the policy and political responses generated by the search for security be understood?	How has the relationship between security and insecurity been expressed in social welfare and crime control policy?	In what ways does the pursuit of security sometimes enhance a sense of insecurity?
Global health regimes (Chapter 5, Section 3)				Looking at the example of HIV/AIDS from Chapter 5, a protective desire to eradicate the disease in developing countries can translate into a narrow and even punitive response, thus possibly making it more difficult to counter the biological and social causes of the disease effectively. In this way it increases insecurity for populations affected by the disease and by wider patterns of infection

Comment

Table 6.1 tries to cover only a small number of the cases that are discussed in the chapters of the book. You may wish to think about how the same questions relate to some of the others (such as gated communities, antisocial behaviour, or war). But even with the limited number of cases that have been considered, it should be clear that there are important relationships between the answers you have included in the different columns. Above all, it should be apparent how entangled the worlds of crime control and welfare are in practice, as well as how social change and policy interact, reinforce and redefine each other. The tension between punitive responses and those couched in terms of social protection runs through the columns, particularly in answer to the third question, but what is also noticeable is that they may coexist uneasily in particular policy initiatives, with the failure of one calling forth the need for the other.

In the next section we want to develop these points further, by focusing directly on the questions and reflecting on the answers that flow from the discussions earlier in the book.

2 Looking for some answers

We think it is possible to draw some tentative conclusions along the lines outlined below.

2.1 Why has security become such an important idea and how does the concept of security link the different domains of social, personal and political life, and especially the worlds of crime control and welfare?

To some degree, the idea that insecurity and fear are driven by social change seems obvious. Throughout this book, the chapter authors have noted some of the key drivers of insecurity, which range from economic precariousness to increasing global instability reflected through conflict and the spread of disease. Governments are also keen to acknowledge that the nature of society has been transformed in recent years. So, for example, the speech of John Reid, who was UK Home Secretary in 2006 (which is quoted in Chapter 1, Section 2), highlights the social fears of crime, antisocial behaviour and terrorism alongside (and in some analyses as a consequence of) the social and cultural impact of globalisation and international migration. The chapters of this book, however, have also considered other ways of thinking about the relationship between insecurity and social change, and how it is shaping the relationship between welfare and crime control policy.

Activity 6.2

In Chapter 1 (Section 3), we noted Jock Young's argument that insecurity arose from a disjuncture between *cultural inclusion* and *structural exclusion* in a variety of different ways depending on the particular position of social groups (Young, 1999, 2007). He suggests that an increased feeling of insecurity and unsettlement in turn leads to cultural and attitudinal changes. These include resentment amongst the relatively deprived (those who can see the possibilities for wealth and social advancement in society but who are denied it in practice, and hence who may resort to crime), and resentment from those on the borderlines of affluence (who experience financial insecurity but also are offered no systems of support) against the deprived and the affluent. Meanwhile, the affluent mobilise their financial wealth to protect themselves against the threats of deprivation and crime emanating from the deprived.

Here, we would like you to consider this argument in the context of the following cases discussed in other chapters. (We have identified where the cases are reviewed in the chapters, just in case you want to remind yourself of them, but the broad argument should be familiar to you.)

■ Gated communities (Chapter 2, Section 3.1)

■ Parenting Orders (Chapter 3, Section 5.2)

■ Anti-social Behaviour Orders (ASBOs) (Chapter 4, Section 2).

Comment

The first case is relatively straightforward. The desire to live in a gated development clearly accords with strategies exercised by the affluent to insulate themselves from perceived threats, although it should be noted that gated developments are not the only means by which this occurs. Within most large cities, particular areas have become insulated from others through a diverse series of practices ranging from the spatial layout of streets that afford a degree of insularity, to high house prices and shops and cafes selling luxury goods. In almost every city the residents know the ways in which these divisions work, where they feel at home and where they feel uneasy or excluded. It should also be noted that, as Young argues, those who are very affluent and mobile tend to be more relaxed about the promises and difficulties of social diversity because they are not so directly affected by them. What is evident, however, is that – as you saw in Chapter 2 – the phenomenon of 'urban villages' or gated developments generally reflects market-based strategies mobilised by social groups to protect themselves against threats to their security.

Figure 6.1
Enjoying the sun in an urban village

Both Parenting Orders, which Jane McCarthy examined in Chapter 3 (Section 5.2), and antisocial behaviour legislation, explored by John Muncie and Ross Fergusson in Chapter 4 (Section 2), are policies developed by government with the aim of dealing with specific social problems. The parenting skills of the poor or of single mothers have come under a great deal of scrutiny by those who fear a breakdown in cultural values and the impact this may have on children. Similarly, antisocial behaviour has provoked a great deal of anger in society because it subjects many people – that is, those unable to protect themselves from it – to annoying or even dangerous behaviours. Many people therefore experience too closely the pressure of family breakdown, poor behaviour or crime, and as a result tend to be supportive of measures designed to contain them. This is what Young (2007) seeks to capture in the notion of 'punitiveness' and Garland (2001) identifies as a 'culture of control'.

So far, we have uncritically presented Young's argument, which points to a generalised punitive trend. Elsewhere in the book, it has been suggested that matters may be rather less straightforward or definite. It is worth considering some evidence which points in different directions, or works to modify the trend. So, for example, the discussion of gated communities in Chapter 2 suggests that even those living within them do not adopt a punitive approach; while the discussions around child protection and family policy in Chapter 3 highlight the mix of socially protectionist and potentially punitive interventions. Even initiatives more centrally located in the arena of crime control policy (such as restorative justice) imply a rather different set of relationships. All of these examples point to the possibility of more ambiguous responses to the variety of pressures people experience.

2.2 Why do people and governments invest so much in the pursuit of different forms of security? How might we understand the types of policy and political responses that are generated by the search for security?

Chapter 1 looked at two examples of the ways in which individuals have attempted to control the perceived threats facing them. First, Section 4.2 looked at preventative strategies such as CCTV, 'designing out crime', and Neighbourhood Watch schemes, or – as you saw in Chapter 2 – attempting to predict what spaces might be 'risky', and thus avoiding the public house with blacked-out windows, which speaks in popular parlance of a 'locals" pub where outsiders might not be welcome. Second, Section 4.3 of Chapter 1 looked at the ways in which individuals seek to manage their own risk by maintaining a respectable face of creditworthiness and home ownership, supported by banks and insurance companies. Chapter 2 considered individualised strategies associated with gated communities and sports utility vehicles, and Chapter 3 reminded us of the extent to which families are seen as safe spaces for family members and also as spaces within which individuals are taught to behave, even if it is in families that child abuse and domestic violence take place.

Many of the strategies pursued by individuals as a consequence of changing economic and social conditions are also directly underpinned by policy, partly through a process of what has been called 'responsibilisation' and partly through direct forms of intervention. So, for example, as you saw in Chapter 1, the rush to secure a private home was prompted both by disillusionment with council housing and also by the gradual erosion of public housing stock, while crime prevention measures are supported and promoted by local government and police forces (see **Hughes, 2009**). Government activity encourages us to 'help ourselves' (encouraging a process of self-governance; see **Clarke, 2008**), although, as you have seen in the case of the extension of home ownership, such privatised strategies may also increase insecurity and anxiety (see Chapter 1, Section 4.3 and Activity 1.6).

Policies aimed at delivering security find a range of expressions as they are directed at different sections of society. So far, we have focused broadly on the mixture of individual and governmental strategies which shape the lives of those in paid employment or with access to reasonable income. For those outside of this majority category – the permanently unemployed, those on welfare, those who have committed an offence or string of offences, those perceived as engaging in antisocial behaviour, or troubled families – a whole range of strategies has been introduced to control, contain and reform. Welfare-to-work, Parenting Orders, Anti-social Behaviour Orders (ASBOs), and toughening attitudes towards prisons and imprisonment are all examples where punitivity can find expression in policy and particular social groups are seen as in some way deficient. For example, in Chapter 3 Jane McCarthy highlighted the ways in which some families are identified as places within which poor parenting may reproduce not only social exclusion but also young people whose behaviour is threatening and socially disruptive.

However, attempts to regulate problem behaviour are not just punitive and containing. Chapter 3 also set out the ways in which family policy is defined through a mix of support and disciplinary intervention. Sometimes apparently punitive initiatives, associated with the threat of legal constraint and punishment, may themselves represent attempts to deliver other forms of social protection. The example of hate crime in Chapter 4 (Sections 3 and 4), and the protocols intended to protect civilians in war, explored in Chapter 5 (Section 2.3), are both examples of an expanding juridical sphere in which attempts have been made, albeit with compromises, to protect civil and human rights.

In effect, therefore, we can say that individual responses to insecurity are enhanced by policy responses, which in turn alter and shape people's behaviour and attitudes.

2.3 How do we make sense of the changing nature of the relationship between security and insecurity, as expressed in social welfare and crime control policy?

In many ways this question has been at the heart of the discussions in the chapters of the book. Each of them in its different way has had this issue at its core. The issue is explicitly explored in Chapter 1 and taken further in the discussions of policy development that are pursued in the following chapters. This is perhaps particularly clear in Chapters 3 and 4.

Activity 6.3

Chapter 3 discusses a range of policies that are centred on families, and Chapter 4 considers new ways of managing conduct in the arena of crime control. Try to list the various ways in which welfare and crime control policy overlap or slide into one another in the two cases. Is this resulting in a more punitive or a more socially protective stance in policy and practice?

Comment

Chapter 3's focus on families is one that is associated with more traditional forms of welfare, while Chapter 4 is apparently more directly focused on issues relating to crime control. Yet it is apparent in each case that the arguments, justifications and practices associated with policy in these areas cannot be so easily distinguished. The support provided to families and to parents, particularly in targeted form, is explicitly directed towards the management of parents whose behaviour puts their children at risk. The process moves seamlessly between financial and other forms of care – from the offer of training programmes aimed at improving behaviour, to the requirement to undertake such programmes, to the removal of children deemed to be 'at risk', to the prosecution of parents identified as being guilty of abuse. Similarly, with children in families, the process moves across a range of policy interventions: from the provision of additional support (from nursery care to free school meals) to the identification of children as being potentially 'risky' or exhibiting 'risky' behaviour – that is, antisocial or criminal behaviour. Once children or young people are identified in this way, the forms of intervention also move easily across a disciplinary spectrum, through an emphasis on self-discipline (or 'responsibilisation') towards criminalisation.

In Chapter 4, the emphasis is more clearly placed on the process of managing antisocial and criminal behaviour, but it is also clear that this cannot simply be reduced to a narrow understanding of crime control. Ross Fergusson and John Muncie explore the ways in which welfarist understandings – or understandings that focus on improving the position of those deemed to behave in antisocial ways – also imbue these interventions. Their discussion of juridification highlights the way in which sets of regulatory frameworks shape understandings of welfare, but also bring such issues much more directly into debates around crime control. In this sense it reminds us of the distinction made by Garland (2001) between prevention and punitivity, which was introduced in Chapter 1, Section 4. The management of antisocial behaviour is in essence a preventative strategy, which allows for intervention in problem behaviour before it becomes criminal. It is also punitive, because failure to comply with an Anti-social Behaviour Order can precipitate criminal prosecution. In some cases, however, being given an Anti-social Behaviour Order can also initiate welfarist interventions.

The notion of hate crime, in rather more complex ways, also raises questions in this context. It promises to criminalise certain unacceptable forms of behaviour motivated by hatred of certain social groups. In essence it aims to improve the welfare of vulnerable members of society, while in practice recognising that it is difficult to pursue prosecution effectively, so that the main claim made for it is that it changes the rules of social behaviour and, in so doing, aims to provide protection for people who are members of minority ethnic groups.

The complex relationship between welfare and crime control is also apparent in the discussion of restorative justice (RJ) in Chapter 4 (Section 5.2). Indeed, here the two aspects of the process seem fundamentally linked. The judicial and criminal justice process appears to dominate, since it is only as part of that process that the relevant negotiations between the victim and perpetrator are undertaken. But RJ is also understood to offer two additional and quite distinctive benefits, which go beyond notions of punishment and criminalisation. The first relates to those identified as victims of crime. For them, restorative justice promises increased welfare, which is demonstrated both by forms of compensatory activity undertaken by those who have undertaken criminal acts and through the act of reconciliation, atonement and forgiveness. The second relates to those identified as criminals, who are expected to benefit from the process of social interaction and recognise the effects of their behaviour on others. In that sense, RJ can be seen as a (more disciplinary or punitive) version of citizenship classes in schools or the training support offered to parents and others as they seek to develop necessary social skills.

None of this should be taken to imply that these are straightforward and unproblematic processes in which welfare and crime control policy are brought easily together. On the contrary, the tensions and conflicts associated with them are also apparent, and the balance between them may differ significantly between policy areas as well as between countries. In Chapters 1 and 2, for example, some of the differences between the UK, European and US experiences are discussed. Similar tensions are highlighted in Chapter 5 in the discussion of the relationship between forms of 'national' and 'human' security. Each may seem to be searching for some sort of social guarantee for particular populations, but they do so from quite different perspectives: the first (which can be seen to start from a crime control perspective) looks for ways of controlling, managing and identifying risk; the second suggests that it is only by providing a wider basis for the well-being of populations that the threats of terrorism and the impact of wars can be minimised. In the case of HIV/AIDS the tensions are particularly clear. The coming together of policies targeted at improving the position of those suffering from or at risk of contracting HIV/AIDS in the countries of Africa and Asia is combined with an approach that tends to blame those who are at risk. This translates itself into campaigns directed at changing behaviour, alongside limited programmes of medical treatment, and in a context which seeks to maintain a protective barrier between those at greatest risk in the poor countries of the world and those living in the richer countries of the world.

2.4 Why do the measures pursued to provide security often not deliver it – indeed, instead often seem to enhance a sense of insecurity?

This is a theme explored across all the chapters of the book. At its simplest, it is perhaps pretty clear that the development of privately marketed security strategies (e.g. in the form of the gated communities or sports utility vehicles discussed in Chapter 2) or the development of public policy initiatives (e.g. in the form of antisocial behaviour initiatives discussed in Chapter 4 or the justifications for military action discussed in Chapter 5) are only possible if particular emphasis is placed on the threat of insecurity in a range of promotional and political campaigning. In other words, once security is identified as a policy or marketing target, it is hardly surprising if the existence of insecurity becomes increasingly taken for granted as the problem against which action has to be taken. A society predicated on the search for security, it might be concluded, is one in which insecurity must be assumed to be a daily fact of life.

Figure 6.2
A selection of headlines from one day's newspapers

This does not mean, however, that insecurity is merely the product of private and political security rhetoric. As Chapter 1 emphasised, feelings of uncertainty are deeply rooted in contemporary social experience; they are not just the product of some malign conspiracy imposed from above. And the ways in which security and insecurity are interrelated and enmeshed are more complex than any such conclusion might imply.

Here we want to return to just a few of the ways in which these points have been explored in the book's chapters, but you may wish to return to consider others.

The examples of gated communities and sports utility vehicles, explored in Chapter 2, focus on the way in which they are promoted and sold. SUVs seem to offer protected spaces (analogous to the security looked for in privately owned housing and gated communities). They are mobile protected spaces, to the extent that (as Graham and Marvin, 2001, note) they help to construct a 'splintered' urbanism as different classes and social groups are able to move in separated spheres of existence defined by the protected space which they carry along with them. At one extreme it might be argued that those protected by SUVs and gated communities are indeed secure, never being challenged by those outside a very narrow circle. However, it is also apparent that such a model is unsustainable. Those within the protected spaces are involved in a constant process of upgrading, precisely because they are so separated and threatened by those on the outside, about whom they know so little and who, therefore, become the objects of fear. In the case of SUVs, in particular, the protected may become targets, precisely because they seem to flaunt their associated wealth and exclusiveness – the very act of building protective spaces suggests that those doing so have something to protect. The model of living implied by the process is one in which the notion of shared 'community' is explicitly undermined (as it becomes restricted to family and friends) and the claims of social justice are ignored, precisely because such claims would bring challenges to the resources which provide security for those behind the wheels of the vehicles or the walls of the gated communities (for more extensive discussion in relation to social justice, see **Newman and Yeates, 2008**; and for more extensive discussion of issues relating to community, see **Mooney and Neal, 2009**).

In Chapter 4, the processes involved in the management of antisocial behaviour raise rather different issues. In this case, the search for security is understood explicitly in terms of challenging the incivility of those who are seen to behave inappropriately – making collective living unpleasant and ultimately engaging in criminal behaviour. Here policy initiatives focus on encouraging or requiring those threatening to undermine the security of the majority to behave differently – the techniques used combine regulation, punitivity and (in some cases) education and training. Here, too, however, the justification for intervention makes it necessary to emphasise the threat involved and – as Chapter 4 indicates – to identify a particular population as essentially threatening. It becomes difficult to see how policy can actually remove the threat, because policy itself is in a constant search for ranges of behaviour that society may find distressing or intimidating.

The cases explored in Chapter 5, those of war and disease, perhaps provide the most compelling examples of how the pursuit of security can generate insecurity. In the process of trying to establish national or global security a diverse set of social problems can be unleashed on societies, ranging from collapsing infrastructures to the spread of infectious diseases. As you also saw, affluent societies are not immune from the fallout from these conflicts, whether this is through increased violence or the global spread of disease. The purpose of the concept of human security is essentially to try to establish those connections, and outline the precondition for *actual* security. As with all the cases we have looked at, however, the search for security interacts with social inequalities, so that security measures are often enacted for the purposes of bolstering one section of society against another, or one country against another. The irony is that the, often simplistic, search for security exemplified in crime control rhetoric may expand the realm of insecurity for both the affluent and the marginalised.

3 Thinking about evidence

The search for answers to the questions about security along the lines developed in Activity 6.1 and in the previous section highlights the need to find convincing forms of evidence to support them. The precise way in which social protection and crime control come together in the context of particular policy initiatives can be understood only with the help of a careful review of the available evidence. The nature of the evidence that might be useful and relevant has been a continuing concern running through the book. We want to focus on those issues in this section.

A wide range of different sorts of evidence has been used in this book. The forms of evidence include:

- various texts which you were encouraged to analyse (e.g. speeches in Chapter 1, advertisements in Chapter 2, official documents in Chapters 3 and 5)

- statistical data (e.g. relating to prisons and mental illness in Chapter 1, hate crime and incivility in Chapter 4, and maps and charts of disease in Chapter 5)

- policy evaluation (e.g. of the Dundee project in Chapter 3)

- personal experience (e.g. relating to families in Chapter 4)

- qualitative evidence from interviews (e.g. relating to risk assessment in Chapter 1, and to gated communities in Chapter 2).

Throughout the chapters you were presented with a series of examples and case studies, as well as references to reports and academic publications to underpin and help you to assess the arguments being presented.

At this stage we just want to distinguish between two different roles which evidence might perform. The first relates to the way in which evidence helps us to understand and explore the relationship between social change and the development of public policy, whether more broadly focused on social (or welfare) concerns or associated with crime control. This is, perhaps, a classically academic approach to evidence. We want to use it to understand and explain what is happening and, if possible, why.

The second role for evidence relates to the way in which it has been or might be used to inform and shape policy. Here what interests us is to see how evidence might be collected and mobilised to develop initiatives capable of delivering particular policy objectives (and might even be used to shape those objectives). Of course, this is not a distinction that can always be sustained consistently, since one might hope (and perhaps even expect) that evidence of the first sort (concerned with understanding) might also feed into policy development. And – equally clearly – the process of policy development is itself something that is often subjected to critical analysis. If this does not sound too circular, it provides evidence to those of us seeking to understand whether, how and what sort of evidence is being used to inform policymaking.

3.1 Qualitative and quantitative evidence and policy development

Both qualitative and quantitative evidence have important contributions to make in the process of investigating social phenomena, although they are often seen as offering competing perspectives.

Briefly, the former involves face-to-face or interactive research that aims to uncover people's perspectives, the meanings they bring to situations, and their subjective understandings. Examples of qualitative research discussed in earlier chapters include:

- Barron's work (discussed in Chapter 1, Section 4.2), which investigated the impact of risk assessment on the identity and development of young female offenders (Barron, 2007)

- Talbot's research (discussed in Chapter 1, Section 4.4) on the experience of regulators and the regulated in the night-time economy (Talbot, 2007)

■ Low's research (discussed in Chapter 2, Section 3.1) on residents' motivations for living in, and their experiences of, gated communities (Low, 2003).

Quantitative evidence, on the other hand, is statistical data which makes it possible to investigate trends over time and tends to aggregate respondents into particular groups, rather than focus on individual experiences. Quantitative evidence may be drawn from government surveys (such as censuses) or other official data (e.g. about levels of employment or the incidence of particular diseases), but surveys can also be undertaken by other agencies and academic researchers. So, for example, Chapter 1 looked at figures relating to imprisonment and psychiatric illness (Section 4.1), Chapter 4 examined the collection of statistics on hate crime and antisocial behaviour (Section 4), while Chapter 5 looked at statistical data on poverty, HIV/AIDS and the human casualties of war.

The evidence generated from the research conducted in each of the cases might be relevant to policy development. So, for example, Barron's research might enable prison reformers to campaign for and institute a more appropriate prison regime for vulnerable young offenders; Talbot's research could lead to a rethink of licensing practice in ways that prioritise the voice of local communities in the process; while, by questioning the underlying philosophy of gated communities, Low's research might be expected to influence planning and housing policy. Similarly, understanding the relationship between psychiatric illness and imprisonment or between poverty and HIV/AIDS, or the charting of an increased incidence of civilian casualties of war, might be expected to be drawn on in the process of policy development. However, the route from research to policy is not an easy one, and neither the marshalling of (apparently harder) statistical data nor the development of (apparently softer) qualitative evidence necessarily feeds directly into policy initiatives.

Governments (and civil servants) certainly do seek to draw on available evidence in developing policy, but the process by which they do so itself requires careful analysis. Explicit statements have been made which emphasise the need for 'better use of available research to design policy, but also extending our knowledge through pilots and robust evaluation studies' (Social Exclusion Unit, 2004, p. 31). And we have certainly become accustomed to seeing major policy initiatives being introduced on the back of new crime statistics relating to anything from knife crime to credit card 'skimming'. However, this merely highlights some of the ambiguities. As Chapter 4 illustrates, crime statistics may give a misleading impression of the direction or extent of change, because of the ways in which they are collected, and particularly as they are amplified through the reports of the mass media. This is reflected in the intense debates that often accompany the latest release of statistics and the attempt to balance different sources (crime recorded by police versus crime identified through surveys).

3.2 Evidence and policymaking

Here we want to return to a few examples from earlier chapters of how research and policy interact, and to consider some of the tensions in the way in which evidence is used in the policymaking process. These are just examples, and you should be able to use a similar approach in considering other cases discussed in the book. We focus on two examples of the importance of the ways in which evidence is interpreted in the policymaking process; as Ross Fergusson and John Muncie point out in Chapter 4, the facts do not speak for themselves.

The first example relates to military conflict. In Chapter 5 (Section 2.2), you were presented with extracts from a classified document prepared by the US Defence Intelligence Agency (DIA, 1991) in 1991 before the first Gulf War. The report focused on the vulnerability of water treatment plants in Iraq, highlighting the extent to which the civilian population of the country was dependent on them as a source of clean water and noting the danger of epidemic diseases if clean water was not available.

This is a piece of research whose purpose was directly intended to influence or inform policy – in this case, presumably military policy. Here, however, the same evidence might be used to support more than one policy. Arguably (if one were following the policy direction associated with human security) the appropriate response of international agencies might be to find means of ensuring that the water treatment facilities in Iraq were maintained. However, if the context for collecting this evidence were (as, in fact, it was) the planning of war, then the policy conclusion would lead the military planners to take advantage of these vulnerabilities, at least if that were deemed to be an acceptable way of pursuing warfare in the context of the very different reality and landscape of contemporary conflict.

The second example relates to work associated with the development of policies directed towards improving parenting in families where children are deemed to be 'at risk'. In Chapter 3 (Section 5.1), Jane McCarthy reports on a piece of work, undertaken by Garrett (2007), that reviewed the Dundee Families Project, which focused on targeted intervention on 'problem families'. This was a project that was predicated on the belief that it is possible through intensive, residentially based, intervention to transform failing families into successful families, ensuring that they provide a context within which children, but also their parents, can thrive.

McCarthy highlights some of the difficulties faced in evaluating policy effectiveness in the context of complex social processes; yet those difficulties are rarely taken significantly into account in policy development. She notes the pressures that face researchers and those evaluating policy initiatives, precisely because what is wanted by policymakers are clear and simple answers, which can be translated into practice. And in this case, it is also apparent that the starting point of policy development has already been framed by some significant parameters. The policies being evaluated already (by implication at least) assume that what is needed is personalised or targeted intervention – policies that might be oriented towards generalised welfare through income support are not considered in this context. In the case discussed in the chapter, the argument that parental behaviour can be transformed by such intervention (as indeed it can in some cases) is translated into a policy which sees that as its main, overriding objective, as reflected in the pages of the UK Government Green Paper *Every Child Matters*. The chapter goes on to consider some of the problems of such a single-minded focus, when other factors may also need to be taken into account.

There are inevitable tensions within any research process that is so closely related to implementation. This was recognised some time ago by Marris and Rein, who concluded from their own research on the policy process that:

> Research requires a clear and constant purpose, which both defines and precedes the choice of means; that the means be exactly and consistently followed; and that no revision takes place until the sequence of steps is completed. Action is tentative, non-committal and adaptive. It concentrates upon the next step, breaking the sequence into discrete, manageable decisions. ... Research cannot interpret the present until it knows the answers to its ultimate questions. Action cannot foresee what questions to ask until it has interpreted the present.
>
> (Marris and Rein, 1972, p. 205)

In other words, even if it is clearly preferable to have some evidence which can inform the process of adaptive action, the nature of that evidence will always itself be uncertain and subject to challenge and reinterpretation.

4 Welfare, crime and security

This book has sought to explore the complex entanglements associated with policies of welfare and crime control in the context of wider concerns with, and initiatives relating to, security. It has done so by setting a wider social context for the processes of change underpinning the rise of security as a policy issue (particularly in Chapter 1, but also in Chapter 2), before considering particular sites where the notions of security and insecurity have a strong resonance in social and policy terms. In Chapter 2, Yvonne Jewkes considered ways in which people have sought to construct their own protected spaces; in Chapter 3, Jane McCarthy reflected on the tensions associated with families as spaces of security and insecurity and the ways in which they have shaped policy; in Chapter 4, Ross Fergusson and John Muncie interrogated the rise of crime control and juridification as ways of shaping and reshaping individual and collective behaviour; and in Chapter 5, we explored the clash between the search for human security and national security in a global context.

In this final chapter, we have focused on a set of key questions first set out in Chapter 1, to which we have now returned, with the benefit of the discussions of the previous chapters. As indicated, we believe that it is possible to draw some tentative conclusions in answer to the questions, but – above all – we hope that we have shown that what matters is the way in which evidence may be used to engage with them. Any answers that we come up with rely upon the careful weighing up of different sources of evidence with the help of critical engagement informed by the wider debates which have helped to frame the questions themselves, as well as upon the nature of the evidence that is relevant in answering them.

References

Barron, C. (2007) 'A paradigm of exclusion: the impact of the risk society on female young offenders' in Law Commission of Canada (ed.) *Risk and Trust: Including or Excluding Citizens*, Black Point, NS, Fernwood.

Clarke, J. (2008) 'Looking for social justice: welfare states and beyond' in Newman, J. and Yeates, N. (eds) *Social Justice: Welfare, Crime and Society*, Maidenhead, Open University Press/Milton Keynes, The Open University.

Defence Intelligence Agency (DIA) (1991) 'Iraq water treatment vulnerabilities' [online] http://www.gulflink.osd.mil/declassdocs/dia/19950901/950901_511rept_91.html (Accessed 12 December 2007).

Garland, D. (2001) *The Culture of Control: Crime and Order in Contemporary Society*, Oxford, Oxford University Press.

Garrett, P.M. (2007) '"Sinbin" solutions: the "pioneer" projects for "problem families" and the forgetfulness of social policy research', *Critical Social Policy*, vol. 27, no. 2, pp. 203–30.

Graham, S. and Marvin, S. (2001) *Splintering Urbanism: Networked Infrastructures, Technological Mobilities and the Urban Condition*, London, Routledge.

Hughes, G. (2009) 'Community safety and the governance of "problem" populations' in Mooney, G. and Neal, S. (eds) *Community: Welfare, Crime and Society,* Maidenhead, Open University Press/Milton Keynes, The Open University.

Low, S. (2003) *Behind the Gates: Life, Security and the Pursuit of Happiness in Fortress America*, New York, NY, Routledge.

Marris, P. and Rein, M. (1972) *Dilemmas of Social Reform: Poverty and Community Action in the United States* (2nd edn), London, Routledge and Kegan Paul.

Mooney, G. and Neal, S. (eds) (2009) *Community: Welfare, Crime and Society,* Maidenhead, Open University Press/Milton Keynes, The Open University.

Newman, J. and Yeates, N. (eds) (2008) *Social Justice: Welfare, Crime and Society,* Maidenhead, Open University Press/Milton Keynes, The Open University.

Social Exclusion Unit (2004) *Breaking the Cycle: Taking Stock of Progress and Priorities*, London, Office of the Deputy Prime Minister.

Talbot, D. (2007) *Regulating the Night: Race, Culture and Exclusion in the Making of the Night-time Economy*, Aldershot, Ashgate.

Young, J. (1999) *The Exclusive Society: Social Exclusion, Crime and Difference in Late Modernity*, London, Sage.

Young, J. (2007) *The Vertigo of Late Modernity*, London, Sage.

Acknowledgements

Grateful acknowledgement is made to the following sources:

Cover

Copyright © Brian David Stevens/Corbis.

Chapter 1

Text

Extract 1.2: Sen, A. (2000) 'Why human security?', Copyright © Amartya Sen.

Tables

Table 1.1: Singleton, N. et al. (1997) *Psychiatric Morbidity Among Prisoners: Summary Report*, Social Survey Division of ONS on behalf of the Department of Health. Crown copyright material is reproduced under Class Licence Number C01W0000065 with the permission of the Controller of HMSO and the Queen's Printer for Scotland.

Figures

Figure 1.1: Copyright © Danny Lawson/PA Wire/PA Photos; Figure 1.2 *left:* Copyright © Geoff Moore/Rex Features; Figure 1.2 *centre:* Copyright © Roy Botterell/Corbis; Figure 1.2 *right:* Copyright © Volker Moehrke/ zefa/Corbis; Figure 1.3: Copyright © Yang Liu/Corbis.

Chapter 2

Text

Extract 2.1: Low, S. (2003) *Behind the Gates: Life, Security and the Pursuit of Happiness in Fortress America*, Routledge. Copyright © 2003 by Taylor & Francis Books, Inc.; Extract 2.2: Reproduced with permission from Josh Lauer, 'Driven to extremes: fear of crime and the rise of the sport utility vehicle in the United States', *Crime, Media, Culture*, vol. 1. Copyright © 2005, by permission of Sage Publications Ltd; Extract 2.3: Hensher, P. (2006) 'Gated communities are promoting irrational fears', *The Independent*, 26 September 2006. Copyright © The Independent.

Figures

Figure 2.1: Copyright © Deborah Talbot; Figure 2.2: Copyright © Deborah Talbot; Figure 2.3 *left:* Copyright © Jon Hicks/Corbis; Figure 2.3 *right:* Copyright © Ricky Leaver/Londonstills.com; Figure 2.4: Copyright © Stuart Atkins/Rex Features.

Chapter 3

Figures

Figure 3.1 *top left:* Copyright © Alain Nogues/Sygma/Corbis; Figure 3.1 *top right:* Copyright © Gideon Mendel/Corbis; Figure 3.1 *bottom left:* Copyright © Gideon Mendel/Corbis; Figure 3.1 *bottom right:* Copyright © Tibor Bognar/Corbis; Figure 3.2: Copyright © N. Armstrong Roberts/ Corbis; Figure 3.3: Copyright © Image Source/Rex Features; Figure 3.4 *top left:* Copyright © Abbie Trayler-Smith/Panos; Figure 3.4 *top centre:* Copyright © Gideon Mendel/Corbis; Figure 3.4 *top right:* Copyright © Kevin Dodge/Corbis; Figure 3.4 *bottom left*: Copyright © Stephanie Maze/Corbis; Figure 3.4 *bottom right:* Copyright © Jim Craigmyle/Corbis; Figure 3.5: Copyright © Giacomo Pirozzi/Panos; Figure 3.6: Ronald Grant Archive.

Chapter 4

Tables

Table 4.1: Home Office (2004) *Defining and Measuring Anti-Social Behaviour: Home Office Development and Practice Report*, Home Office, Crown copyright material is reproduced under Class Licence Number C01W0000065 with the permission of the Controller of HMSO and the Queen's Printer for Scotland; Table 4.2: Home Office (2006) *Anti-Social Behaviour Orders*, Home Office Research Development & Statistics Directorate, Crown copyright material is reproduced under Class Licence Number C01W0000065 with the permission of the Controller of HMSO and the Queen's Printer for Scotland; Table 4.3: Scottish Executive (2007) *Statistical Bulletin: Criminal Justice Series – Racist Incidents Recorded by the Police in Scotland, 2003/04 to 2005/06*, Crown copyright material is reproduced under Class Licence Number C01W0000065 with the permission of the Controller of HMSO and the Queen's Printer for Scotland.

Figures

Figure 4.1: Copyright © Terry Cooper; Figure 4.2: Copyright © Stuart Rayner, courtesy of the Riverside Group; Figure 4.3: Copyright © Bettmann/Corbis; Figure 4.4: Copyright © Monika Graff/Getty Images.

Chapter 5

Text

Extract 5.1: Commission on Human Security (2003) *Human Security Now*, Human Security Unit, United Nations.

Figures

Figure 5.1: Copyright © Mahesh Kumar/AP/PA Photos; Figure 5.2: Copyright © Leon Neal/AFP/Getty Images; Figure 5.3 *left:* Copyright © Johnny Green/PA Archive/PA Photos; Figure 5.3 *right:* Copyright © Reuters/Corbis; Figure 5.4: Copyright © Syed Jan Sabawoon/epa/Corbis; Figure 5.5: Copyright © Jerome Delay/AP/PA Photos; Figure 5.7: Copyright © Achim Pohl/Das Fotoarchiv/Still Pictures; Figures 5.8 and 5.9: Copyright © 2006 SASI Group (University of Sheffield) and Mark Newman (University of Michigan) http://www.worldmapper.org.

Chapter 6

Figures

Figure 6.1: Copyright © Alex Segre/Alamy.

Index